COOKING WITH MOM

PAMELA BREALEY

ISBN: 978-1-64184-515-1 (Hardcover)

DEDICATION

To my sons, Justin and Matthew, who were gifted to me. There aren't words to express all the heart feels. It's been an honor to be your mother. To watch you two grow into loving men, husbands and fathers. I'm sure Grandma Rita is looking down with such pride. You gave her so much happiness.

A special thank you, Matt, for all your help with navigating the technical difficulties with getting the book together.

To my brothers, Joe and Tim, who I love with all my heart and for putting up with me all these years. Without you, there wouldn't be a cookbook. Thank you both for taking this Disney ride of life with me.

To my step children, Chelsea and Jason, for the memories we made in that Kirkland kitchen. It was real, wasn't it? I loved being the Brady Bunch. My life has been blessed with the two of you in it.
Love has no boundaries.

Last to my grandchildren, Michael, Clara, Charlotte, Jackson and Jordan. May this book provide you the opportunity to make memories of your own someday. To do little things with great love.

This way great grandma Rita's light will continue to burn brightly. My love will follow you always.

FORWARD

"Do small things with great love."
Mother Theresa

Small things. That's pretty much all my mother, Rita Bruce, had. I believe because mom had so few things while growing up, she developed a keen sense of what really mattered in life. Love. Everything mom did, was done with great love.

That is the purpose of this cookbook. Cooking with great love is all Rita knew. After making her transition in December of 2000, I felt not only a deep emptiness, but, that an era of love left with her. How could someone give so much of those "little things," without leaving something behind for all of us who knew her? With that, my mission became clear. This is a tribute to my mother, this is her legacy.

She would often say, "You get more with honey than with vinegar, and love heals all. And over the years, I learned that she was right. Not that I always got it right. I was known to have a temper and little patience. May I remind you, she spared no feelings in letting me know how unattractive that behavior could be. There were no apologies, just love in her eyes. Often, mom would teach these lessons in the kitchen while we were making dinner. As I look back, I was so blessed to have had those special moments with her. So, I decided to put some of her favorite recipes together and share my memories of making them with her.

In putting this little project together, I could see that the cookbook wasn't really about her recipes. Though, I'm sure some of you will be thrilled to have them. What mom was leaving us was the "memory making" in cooking. It's the time spent with those you love, creating something special, like pies, or delicious cookies. Yes. Through her cooking, she wasn't just nurturing our bodies, she nurtured our spirit. I'm pretty clear that this is what mom wanted to share with all of us.

With many of the recipes I've included here, I've provided a little insight into those ordinary times. Every day occurrences, dinners, desserts, coffee. And mom always had a way of making the "ordinary'" feel special. Life, itself, was special to mom and she didn't like wasting a moment of it.

What I would like all of you to do, is to reconsider "meals". It's actually not about the "food", it's more an opportunity to express love for those you care about, be it a birthday celebration or a little surprise just for fun. Even if it's beans and hotdogs, make it special by baking them with cheddar cheese on top and a sprinkle of love. Then look for the smiles. I know my mother lived for smiles.

I'll leave you with this. It's the time spent with family that meant so much to mom. Your kids will remember what you do with them a lot longer than what you did for them. Make memories with your children, who will grow up and, in turn, share those same memories with their children.

Now it's your turn to invite someone into your own kitchen and dance. Laugh, be silly and bake some cookies! Share your stories. This is how love lives on. As you go through these pages, you will feel Rita's light shining bright within your heart. She lives on with each of us.

COOKING WITH MOM

"The Kitchen"

Remember Mom's (Grandma's) kitchen? The old appliances and those green floor rugs? No matter where she moved, she had a way of creating the same kitchen. Homey and inviting. Oh, and that old chrome toaster? She had it for at least 15 years. We had to press the bread down twice in order get it to toast. But, as long as it still worked, it stayed. Along with the ancient deep fat fryer.

Mom had me scared to death of that fryer at a very young age. Each time she pulled it from the cupboard, I was reminded of the harm all that hot grease would do if I got too close. And then one day, she actually told me a story that created enough fear in me that I decided then and there that I would never own one. Justin and Matt, that explains why only grandma had one.

The countertops were always spotlessly clean. I can still smell the Pine Sol on the floors. Comet, Joy and SOS pads were among the required cleaning items under her sink.
She'd stand at the sink, fingers in scaling hot water, washing the dishes. I'd watch and wonder why her fingers weren't burnt. The only dishwasher we had while growing up was mom, or when appointed, one of us three.

Then there were those times when I'd wake up early and find mom on her hands and knees, washing the kitchen floor, smelling like Pine Sol. Not exactly sure why she continued to do the floor by hand. Maybe to get closer to the dirt in the corners? I must have been in my teens before I realized other people used a mop.

Think back to that ever so important stove. That old wooden hen she kept perched on the top. She kept it all those years because she liked reading the verse on it. "I put all my eggs in one basket, then I give

my basket to God". I think we can all agree, that verse is a refection of the way mom lived her entire life. She carried such a strong faith. And, next to the hen sat that very old china ring dish, a gift from us. It had to be 30 years old. She never gave anything away that she loved, no matter how many times she had to glue it back together. Like those 2 overly glued spoon rests that Aunt Lois gave her, sitting in the middle of the stovetop. They dated back to the 1970's, along with those mason jar salt and pepper shakers.

Just above the stove, and under the hood vent, hung a print of a majestic sunrise, with "Praise the Lord" hand painted on it. Remember how curious we were about mom's Southern Baptist roots? She rarely attended church with us. I'm not sure she attended any while growing up either. Still, she had an unwavering faith and the belief that "Jesus died on the cross for all of us." How many times did we three hear "God didn't make any mistakes"? She was so very proud of her precious children.

Makes me smile as I write this. "My precious angel" is how mom generally referred to me. Hand written in every card she ever gave me. I wonder, now, if my being born without a father, when she was only 17, had anything to do with that. Giving birth without a husband must have been frightening back in 1952. Deep in the South, on a tobacco farm abandoned by the one she loved. She was alone, except for many of her older sisters, suggesting she put the baby up for adoption. She had to have been leaning on her faith when she decided to keep the precious angel. For that, I am eternally grateful. Our mother walked with the grace of God.

Back to the kitchen. The refrigerator flaunted a variety of pictures, primarily family. Mom and Vernon loved the Seattle Times and most days one of them would cut out a "Love is…" poem, or one of those "household hint" articles. Oh, the weekly menu. It too, was posted on the side of the refrigerator. Planning a weekly menu was a task that mom and Vern enjoyed doing together.

How much did mom love her flowers? The purple blooming African violets sitting on the kitchen windowsill. I loved those. Mom explained to me that in order for African violets to bloom, you needed two. A

male and a female, then they would mate and produce flowers. I have no idea which is which, but when I buy two, they bloom.

Mom planted a flower garden every year. In the yard and/or in pots. I'm not sure, but I think geraniums were her favorite. There were so many varieties and colors. She taught us all how important "dead heading" was to the continued blooming process. Most Saturdays, during the late spring and summer, we would find her at the local nurseries. That big, blue, Dodge pickup loaded with all kinds of plants. Then, Sunday, mom would head over to Aunt Lois's with a bed full of blooming flowers. Before leaving, she'd tell me just how much work it was to help her sister plant them. That's because mom planted while Lois sat and talked. Yet, no matter the long distance or her aching back, she would still look forward to returning the following week. On that note, remember how mom would laugh when she told us that Lois came to visit, just to hold down the living room chair?

Those old, rusted black iron wall planters holding overgrown ivy were hanging in every house we ever lived. At least as far back as I can remember. That ivy grew for some 40 years, I think. Mom had a green thumb for sure. It was no surprise, on the last Sunday she was home, our mother insisted that the ivy be watered. And, no thank you, she didn't want help. We watched as she walked the room with one hand on the wall, keeping her balance. Somehow, she managed to get up on her tiptoes and stretch just enough to get it done.

The walls of the kitchen were colored with pictures of all those she loved, along with spiritual and religious prints. Reminding mom and anyone else in the room that God loved us, and to never loose faith.

Mom's style of decor wasn't extravagant. It was more like country chic and there was no place like it. Always felt warm and cozy. Full of treasures she refused to part with. In fact, after mom died, we found stacks and stacks of greeting cards that we had all given her over the span of some 25 years or more. From Vernon, Aunt Lois, other sisters, her children, grandsons and so many friends. Every one of her dresser drawers and night stands were lined with cards. Beautiful memories.

Looking back on those early years when we were really young and living in military housing, I remember things were often difficult and there was very little money. So mom used food and cooking as a way of giving to us. She cooked with love which then made her excited to share whatever it was with us. I'm sure she needed to lift her own spirits as well as ours. She would make a favorite dinner of one of us and then bake a favorite dessert of another. Our mom loved surprises. Giving much more than receiving.

Like that last lemon meringue pie she made the summer before she died. I had flown up from LA to be with her when she found out the results of her biopsy. It was just like mom to bake away the back pain and hide her fear behind the excitement of the surprise. Mom picked me up at SeaTac in that brand new Dodge pickup and we drove straight home. She opened the front door, went to the kitchen, only to return with a big smile and a pie in her hands. Big green eyes beaming, she waited for my expression. In the meringue, she had written "Love to Pam". I'll never see another lemon meringue pie that I won't be reminded of the love she held in her heart that day.

And surprising Tim with his favorite molasses cookies. She made dozens and dozens of them every Christmas and shipped them down to SanDiego along with pounds of beef jerky. Many times complaining about shipping costs as she'd squeeze in another pound of jerky. There were Joe's special chocolate chip pancakes. Mom would make them with silly smiley faces, then run to wake him up with kisses and hugs. They shared a close bond that only mothers and sons can have. When she talked about Joe and Tim you could see her face light up.

From about the age of 7, mom bought Joe a pair of new sneakers for his birthday, December 12th. That annual tradition continued until the year before she died. Joe was 45 and still she took him shopping for his sneaks. He looked forward to it as much as mom did. That last birthday, mom was too ill for shopping. In fact, mom went into the hospital on December 11th that year for the last time. Placed on morphine, reality sunk in. Joe thought her last gift to him was that she would pass on his birthday. As a mother, myself, I knew she wouldn't leave us on his special day, She loved him too much. So,

at 1:36 AM, December 13th, she let go. So fitting. So Rita. The gift she gave to Joe? She waited.

A big part of my own life will never be the same without mom. My own kitchen is lonely and I miss being able to call and ask for a recipe or directions for cooking something. Mostly, just to say "Hi" and "I love you". There were lots of dishes and desserts we called "favorites". That's why I decided to put the recipes she used into a collection for all of us. I figured that if I miss her cooking and baking, you all must too. Plus, there's no better way to feel close to her. Just open the book to any recipe and I'm sure the memories will come flooding back. Mom used to remind me that the time we shared in the kitchen would be "our" memories, and the day would come when I would have to make memories of my own. With my own family. She was right. Blessed with those beautiful, bittersweet memories with mom, the time eventually came when I found myself trying to create those same memories with my sons. Now, I'm passing on her traditions and love of cooking with all of you. I hope that you, too, will make sweet memories cooking with someone you love. Nothing would make mom happier.

Over the years, mom collected hundreds of recipes. Some handed down several generations and others she collected from a variety of publications. Like those days at a doctor's office when I would catch her scrambling through her purse for a scrap of paper to write on. There were no cell phones or laptops back then. Plus, she despised people who ripped the pages out of the magazine. So, as you can imagine, some of these recipes were a bit difficult to make out.

I really hope this cookbook brings memories of times you shared in Mom's Kitchen. Even if you don't use the book for cooking or baking, just reading it will allow you to revisit with her on occasion. You gotta know she's been with me overseeing this little project. Many times, I've heard her voice telling me, "don't double the recipe". This book is not only a collection of her recipes, but a recalling how she cooked with love.

CONTENTS

SIX WEEKS MUFFINS

Preheat oven to 400F
Fill muffin tins with liners

5 teaspoons baking soda
2 cups boiling water
1 cup shortening. Mom used Crisco, but butter might work as well.
2 cups sugar
4 eggs, slightly beaten
1 quart buttermilk
1 tablespoon salt
2 cups dates, chopped
5 cups flour
2 cups 40% Bran Flakes
2 cups All Bran
2 cups walnuts, chopped

In a small sauce pan add baking soda to boiling water and let cool.

Using an electric mixer, cream together shortening and sugar. Beat in eggs quickly. Stir in buttermilk, flour and salt and dates. Add soda water.

In a large mixing bow, combine a cereals, and nuts. Stir liquid batter into dry ingredients until well blended. Fill muffin cups full and bake for 20 to 25 minutes or until done.

Batter can be stored in the refrigerator for up to 6 weeks.

AMBROSIA SALAD

As long as I can remember, mom made this salad for us on holi-days. Truth be told, I don't think she liked it that much. But we did, so she still loved making it for us. After Justin and Matt were born, Grandma continued to make it with extra marshmallows, because her grandsons liked those the most. Every Easter, Thanksgiving, Christmas and New Years it was on the table. And any other day her grandsons wanted it.

RECIPE

2 cans mandarin orange segments, drained
1 large can pineapple chunks, drained
1/2 cup coconut
1 cup miniature marshmallow (2 cups for Justin)
1/2 cup sour cream, optional
1 large container of Cool Whip softened.

In a big bow, mix it all together and serve cold

APPLE MELT

Apples and cheese. Mom ate them together all the time. So when I found this recipe among the others she'd stuffed away, I knew it had to be added to the cookbook. During the fall and winter, she made these baked apples as a treat to herself. On the occasion when she had visitors, like us kids, she'd omit the shredded cheese. While others were topping their apples with vanilla ice cream, mom was topping hers with a big slice of cheddar cheese, and watching it melt as she ate it. Always crossed legged and toes moving in contentment.

As mom added a little love with everything she baked, we should too Especially as these apples are such a comfort food. She used to say, "Everything tastes a little bit better with love added in".

RECIPE

Preheat oven to 350F

4 apples (partially cored, leaving 1/4 inch on the bottom)
I have no idea what kind of apples. I just remember them being red.
I'm guessing they need to be firm and somewhat tart
1/2 cup shredded cheddar cheese
1/4 cup raisins1/4 cup chopped walnuts
1 tablespoon brown sugar
1 teaspoon cinnamon

Mix ingredients together and stuff apples. Bake for 30 minutes.

APPLE PEAR GINGER PIE

This is the last recipe added to this cookbook. It was a suggestion from Uncle Sonny. He had seen an ad for it somewhere and thought the combination of apples, pears and fresh ginger sounded delicious. So, I did some research and found one. I have made two and they were a great hit.

RECIPE

Preheat oven to 350F

Double pie crust

Zest and juice 1 lemon
Peel and core 3 apples, depending on size, about 3 cups. I used both Gala and Granny Smith, but it might be fun to experiment with other varieties.
Peel and core 2 pears, depending on size, about 2 cups. I used Anjou, but agin, you can try another variety
1/2 cup packed brown sugar
1 tablespoon cornstarch
1 tablespoon fresh grated ginger
1/4 teaspoon ground ginger
1 teaspoon cinnamon

Thinly slice pears and apples. Put into a very large mixing bowl. Toss with lemon juice and zest. Add brown sugar, cornstarch, cinnamon and both fresh grated and ground ginger. Toss and mix well.

Pour mixture into a 9 inch unbaked pie crust. Roll remaining crust out and slice 8 one inch slices. Place strips one inch apart over pie. 4 slices in one direction and 4 slices in the other, overlapping to form a lattice. Trim ends and press down the edges with a fork to seal. Trim excess dough.

Brush pie with milk and sprinkle granulated sugar over the entire pie. Bake in preheated over for about 50 minutes, until crust is golden brown and filling bubbles.

Remove from oven and cool.

APPLESAUCE OATMEAL MUFFINS

From what I can read on the handwritten recipe, it looks like you can replace the applesauce with drained canned pineapple, as well as adding nuts or raisins, depending which one you use.

Preheat oven to 400F
Use muffin cups or grease and flour muffin tin.

In a big bowl, mix together the following ingredients and set aside.

1/2 cup brown sugar
1 1/2 cup oats
1 1/2 cup flour
3/4 teaspoon cinnamon
1 teaspoon baking powder
3/4 teaspoon baking soda

In a separate bowl, blend the following ingredients together.

1 cup applesauce
1/2 cup skim milk
3 tablespoons oil
1 egg
1/2 cup raisins or walnuts, if desired.

Fold dry ingredients into batter and spoon into muffin cups.
Bake for 15-20 minutes, or until they spring back when touch and they're golden brown.

HOMEMADE BARBECUE SAUCE

I received this recipe from a co-worker at the Hartford Insurance Group way back in 1972. Well, that makes me feel old now.

I love how easy it is to make and how great it is on chicken and ribs. Plus you can make it ahead of time and store it in the fridge. No cooking required.

2 tablespoons vinegar
2 tablespoons Worcestershire sauce
2 tablespoons sugar
3/4 cup catsup
1 teaspoon salt
1/2 teaspoon black pepper
1/4 teaspoon red pepper
1 teaspoon chili powder
1 teaspoon paprika
1/2 cup water

Combine all ingredients, adding water last. Mix well.

OLD FASHIONED BEEF STEW

On winter, rainy Pacific Northwest days, mom liked make comfort food, like stews, pot roasts and soups. The house would feel so warm and cozy. After simmering all day, the smells lofting from the kitchen. I loved this stew so much and would over eat whenever she served it. Later, a mother of my own, I often made this stew for Justin and Matt on those dark rainy Seattle nights. We enjoyed eating it by the living room fire with a warm loaf of sourdough bread, making our own memories.

Mom found this recipe in a very old "meat cookbook" that she pre-served during all the moving she did. I was so surprised to find it still in tact. Fortunately, I was able to salvage the cherished cookbook and add it to my own collection.

RECIPE

2 pounds beef chuck, cut in 1 inch cubes. (Mom liked to buy a chuck roast and cut the meat herself. Less expensive and less waste.)
1 cup flour
2 tablespoons Crisco (I use oil)
4 cups water, boiling
1 tablespoon lemon juice
1 teaspoon Worcestershire sauce
1 clove garlic, minced
1 medium onion, sliced
2 bay leaves
1 tablespoon salt
1 teaspoon sugar
1/2 teaspoon pepper
1/2 teaspoon paprika
1/4 teaspoon allspice
6 carrots, sliced diagonally
6 potatoes, cut into small quarters

Bring 4 cups water to boil
In a large pot, heat oil.

Spoon flour into a large paper bag, then add meat. Shake well to coat each piece. Add more flour if necessary. Brown meat in hot oil turning as needed. Pour in boiling water. Add lemon juice, Worcestershire sauce, garlic, onion, bay leaves and seasonings. Cover pot and simmer 2 hours.

Remove bay leaves. Add carrots and potatoes. Once again cover and cook for an additional 30 minutes or until the vegetables are tender.

The gravy can be thickened by adding a mixture of 1/2 cup flour with 1/4 cup cold water. Flour mixture must be smooth before adding to the stew.

BOSTON BAKED BEANS

This recipe comes from one of my favorite places in Boston.

Fanuel Hall at Durgin Park Market, I love the family style seating around long picnic tables. When I walked in for lunch as a single, I was placed at a table of other single diners. What a great idea! Such an easy way to meet people from all over the world.

I quickly came to see that there are no other beans like these. I found out that the restaurant actually employs a special cook just for the beans. He's known as "Chief Bean Man". I wanted to ask for the recipe, but I knew that would be a waste of time. And, then, several years later, after moving to Seattle, I was reading a Family Circle magazine and found this recipe under "The Best of the Best" for baked beans. Lucky us!

RECIPE

Preheat oven to 300F
Makes 8 servings

1 package (1 pound) navy or pea beans
6 cups water
1/2 teaspoon baking soda
1/2 pound salt pork, cut into 1/2 inch pieces
1 small onion, chopped
1/3 cup molasses
1/4 cup sugar
1 teaspoon dry mustard
1/4 teaspoon pepper

In a large bowl, place beans in the 6 cups of water. Soak overnight.

Pour beans and water into a large pot and add baking soda. Over high heat bring to boiling. Lower heat and continue to boil slowly for

another 10 minutes. Drain beans into a colander, over a large bowl, in order to preserve liquid.

Place salt pork, onion and beans into a 2 quart bean pot or casserole dish. Combine molasses, sugar, dry mustard, pepper and 1 cup of reserved liquid. Pour over beans and stir thoroughly. Add just enough reserved liquid to cover beans (about a cup).

Cover and bake in prepared oven for about 2 hours. Add remaining liquid, stir thoroughly and continue baking for an additional 1 1/2 to 2 hours, or until beans are tender and liquid is is absorbed. For a thicker consistency, bake uncovered for the last 30 minutes.

RITA'S BRAN MUFFINS

I don't think mom ever slept in. She was up very early every morning like 4:30-5:00. Many of those mornings she spent in the kitchen baking. After we grew up and moved out, she continued the ritual for her husband, Vernon.

She made his lunch every morning. I can't remember her not being in the kitchen when we got up. Always the smells of fresh coffee and something baking in the oven was the air. It made getting out of bed so much easier. Mom in her worn out bathrobe, red hair standing on end. Her inviting sweet smile. I usually found her standing with a cup of coffee in hand, while a cigarette burned in the ashtray, lost in her own world.

As we drank coffee, she'd remind me of how hard Vernon worked in the foundry. His lunches had to sustain him through the day. And, I'm sure they did. Lunch usually consisted of meat sandwiches, cheese, crackers, celery, carrots sticks and a couple of candy bars. She loved to add a fresh muffin or two. These bran muffins were his favorite.

By the time his old beat up lunchbox was sufficiently full, it would barely close. Mom and I would laugh, but she was happy to help keep him energized and healthy. I remember once asking her how he could possibly eat all that food and still have room for dinner when he got home. She smiled and told me the lunchbox always came home empty.

Their routine didn't vary even during their last years together. She would pour a cup of coffee for Vernon, fill our cups and put on another pot for his thermos. Every day for 20 years, she sent him off with a kiss, a thermos full of coffee, and his enormous lunch.

One night after mom's passing, Vern and I shared stories about all the special things mom did for us. And the loving things she did for him. He totally surprised me with how much he loved those lunches, but

he could never eat it all. He would share half of it with his coworkers. Vern said he never had the heart to tell mom that she was making him too much food. So, he just let her continue to make his lunch and he just continued to share it. That's Love.

RECIPE

Preheat oven to 400. Grease muffin tins or use pleated muffin cups.

2 1/2 cups Bran Flakes
1 1/4 cups milk

Mix together and let stand 2 minutes

1 1/4 cups all purpose flour
3 teaspoons baking powder
1/4 cup sugar
1/2 teaspoon slat
1 teaspoon baking soda

Stir together and set aside

1/3 cup vegetable oil
1/4 cup molasses
1/2 cup raisins
1 egg (slightly beaten)

Mix together and add bran flakes. Blend well.

Stir in flour mixture, just until combined. Do not over stir or beat the batter.

Drop by spoonful into each muffin tin. Bake for about 25 minutes, Just until brown on top. Center of muffin should spring back. Do not over bake.

OLD FASHIONED BREAD PUDDING

Well, here's a flashback that dates us all.

The year? 1960. Summertime. We three were living on the military base of Camp Pendleton, CA. We were maybe 3, 5 and 8 years old. Baths and jammies, we would be seated on the cold bare living room floor. That was our daily routine. Our eyes focused on the black and white TV, while we waited.

Our favorite time. Mommy loved to surprise us. And most every night she did. With dessert! This was one of my favorites. Big bowls of pudding topped with cinnamon and whipped cream.

I learned to make it with her. Ripping bread into a large bowl. Another bonding opportunity. As we ripped, she shared her own memories of ripping bread with her mother, Grandma Vic.

Remembering how important that the custard be firm and not watery. And, the milk had to be scalded. Not understanding what scalded meant, mom showed me how to stir the hot milk until it boiled and formed a skin on top. Then, because the milk was so hot, we had to be careful adding the eggs because the hot water would cook them. Always add the eggs a little at a time, stirring quickly.

RECIPE

Preheat oven to 350. Grease a 1 1/2 quart baking dish

2 cups bread cubes. (Great time to use up that dried up bread)
4 cups milk, scalded
1 tablespoon butter
3/4 cup sugar
4 eggs, beaten
1 teaspoon vanilla
1/4 teaspoon cinnamon

1/4 teaspoon nutmeg
1/2 cup raisins

Soak bread crumbs into scalded milk for 5 minutes. Add butter, salt and sugar. Slowly, a little at a time, pour mixture over eggs. Add vanilla spice and raisins. Pour over prepared baking dish.

Place the baking dish into a larger pan with 2 inches hot water. Bake about 40-50 minutes, until the pudding tests firm with a toothpick inserted into the center. Serve warm topped with cinnamon and whipped cream if desired.

BRITISH SHORTBREAD
BY NANNY

Another Brealey favorite. Justin and Matt, I know you remember the nightly cup of tea, just before bed. These cookies were perfect for dunking. As Nanny was British, she loved biscuits and tea. I like them with coffee as well. So easy to make.

REICPE

Preheat oven to 350F
Rolling surface, lightly floured

2 cups butter
1/4 teaspoon vanilla
1 cup powdered sugar
4 cups flour

Cream butter and sugar, then add vanilla. Mix well and add flour, 1 cup at a time, mixing well after each cup. Knead dough until it's smooth and any cracks disappear.

Using the floured surface, roll out dough until it's just about 1/2 inch thick. Cut dough into strips about the size of our fingers, 1"x3".

Bake for about 20-25 minutes. Cool and with a sifter, cover with powdered sugar.

COUNTRY BUTTERMILK BISCUITS

It was so fascinating to watch mom making these little soft puffs of dough. Squishing the Crisco through the flour with her fingers, just looked like so much fun. I'm sure I nagged mom to death to show me how. Must be because the process was so messy. Eventually she gave in and taught me. Just like Grandma Vic teaching her. Most importantly, she showed me how to properly knead the dough. That was my favorite part. It was like playing with Play Doh.

Growing up on the farm and cooking with her mother, mom learned that it was important to take your time and carefully measure everything. She told me over and over that rushing caused mistakes. To her, it wasn't just food, it was her pride, as everything was made by hand.

When Bisquick came to the market. Mom wasn't about to try it. She had always made biscuits from scratch and she wasn't about to stop.

Everything in its own time. Things change, as we all know. Eventually, she realized using the boxed stuff would save so much time, effort and cleanup. Plus they were, well, pretty good.

So, here we are 2020, in the era of instant everything. You can just buy biscuits or use a boxed mix. However, you might want to feel the love when making your own. Try it, it's fun.

And I absolutely loved it when we made them for breakfast! We used to eat them right out of the oven with butter and molasses.

Preheat oven to 400F.

2 cups flour, sifted
2 teaspoons baking powder
1/2 teaspoon baking soda
1/2 teaspoon salt

4 tablespoons shortening **
3/4 cup buttermilk.

**On the farm, mom's mother used lard! Mom advanced to Crisco in the 60's. She swore that shortening made the biscuits lighter.

In a large bowl, sift and measure flour 1 cup at a time to equal 2 cups. Add salt, baking powder and baking soda. Sift again.
Cut in shortening with a pastry blender. Gradually, add buttermilk. Stir with a fork to make a soft dough. Sprinkle a little more flour over dough, rolling into a soft ball.

Pinch a heaping tablespoonfull and roll gently in flour, making small balls. Place on cookie sheet and press biscuits down gently with 2 fingers, about half way down.

Bake for 15 minutes, or until they rise and are golden brown.

BUTTERSCOTCH OATMEAL BLONDIES

Of all the brownies mom made for us, these were by far my favorite.

Preheat oven to 375F
Grease a 9x13 baking pan

2 cups flour
1 1/2 cups old fashioned oats
2 teaspoons baking powder
1 teaspoon salt
1 teaspoon baking soda
2 sticks or 1 cup butter, softened
1 1/2 cups brown sugar
2 eggs, slightly beaten
2 tablespoons milk
2 teaspoons vanilla
1/2 cup chopped walnuts or pecans, optional
1 11-oz bag butterscotch morsels

In a large bow, stir together flour, baking powder, baking soda and salt. Mix in oats and set aside.

In a large mixing bowl, using an electric mixer, blend together the butter and sugar, vanilla, eggs and milk. Continue to beat until creamy.

Add the dry ingredients to the wet mixture and continue beating on low speed until just combined. Stir in the butterscotch chips and nuts.

Spread in prepared baking pan and bake for 20-25 minutes or until just cooked through. Check to see that the top isn't getting too brown. Cover with foil the last 10 minutes if necessary.

Cool completely for easier cutting.

CALICO BAKED BEANS

If you're not into marathon bean cooking, here's a quick, easy and great alternative.

3/4 pound bacon, cut into smaller pieces
3 cups onions, thinly sliced
3/4 cup brown sugar, packed
14 teaspoon dry mustard
1/2 cup catsup
1/4 cup vinegar
1 16 oz can butter beans
1 32 oz can Bushes baked beans
1 pound frozen lima beans

Cook bacon until done but not crispy. Drain, reserving 3 tablespoons drippings.

Put bacon in a large bean pot or crock pot. Add reserved drippings, onions, sugar, mustard, catsup and vinegar. Simmer 20 minutes. Stir in beans and cook slowly for about 30 minutes.

CAPPUCCINO PARFAITS

4 teaspoons instant coffee
1 tablespoon hot water
1 1/2 cups cold milk
1 4 oz box chocolate instant pudding
1/2 teaspoon cinnamon
1 cup cool whip topping
3 chocolate wafer cookies, crushed.

Dissolve coffee in water. Add milk, pudding and cinnamon. Whip with a wire whisk for 2 minutes. Let and for 5 minutes or until pudding is thick. Gently stir in cool whip.

Pour half pudding mixture in 5 dessert glasses/dishes. Sprinkle the crushed cookies on top. Then spread remaining pudding over cookie crumbs. Garnish with whipped topping.

CHEESECAKE

I truly can't recall exactly when or where mom and I found this recipe. I do remember making it with with her when I was first married. We thought this was the best cheesecake recipe ever because it included 5 eggs and a pound of cream cheese! Plus it's so much lighter than others.

Originally, the recipe called for cherry pie filling as a topping. But, years of playing around with it, we found that fresh raspberries were by far the best. Mom and I each tried fresh or frozen strawberries, blueberries, boysenberries and just about every other fruit as toppings and we kept coming back to the raspberries.

A couple of notes here. It's important to beat the egg yolks until they are very dark yellow. Beating for probably 7 or 8 minutes. And, you'll want to have the cream cheese and sour cream at room temperature, or trust me you'll never get the lumps out. Also only use a glass bowl when whipping the egg whites.

And, lastly do not open the oven to see how it's baking! Mom used to say it was like pulling up carrots to see how they're growing.

RECIPE

Preheat oven to 275F and butter a deep dish pie plate.

Crust
1/2 cup graham cracker crumbs
1 tablespoon sugar
1/4 teaspoon nutmeg
1/4 teaspoon cinnamon
Mix together. Sprinkle into prepared pie plate and pat down.
Refrigerate

Cheesecake
5 eggs separated
1 cup sugar
16 oz cream cheese (room temperature)
1 cup sour cream (room temperature)
2 tablespoons flour
1 teaspoon vanilla

Using an electric mixer, beat egg yolks to a very yellow color, 5 to 7 minutes. Beat in sugar until blended. Blend in cream cheese, and then the sour cream. Beat until smooth. Lastly add the flour and vanilla. Continue to beat until batter is smooth. Set aside.

Place the 5 egg whites into a glass mixing bowl. Beat until they form soft peaks firm but not stiff. Do not over beat.

Carefully, with a large clean spatula (free of any oil), fold the egg whites into the batter until mixed. Turn into the refrigerated crust and bake for 70 minutes. Turn off oven and let rest for 1 hour. Again, do not open the oven for the entire time.

When completely cool frost the cheesecake with any fruit glaze.

Glaze
Pour enough fruit juice from can to make 1 cup. If not enough juice add water to the juice to make a cup. Add 2 tablespoons cornstarch. Bring to a boil until mixture is clear and thick. Mix in fresh, frozen or canned fruit. Spoon onto the cheesecake.

CHICKEN CACCIATORE

This is a little different cacciatore than the standard Italian recipe. Mom and I found it in a "Cooking Light" cookbook. We loved the flavor and found it lighter than other recipes. This was the winner.

RECIPE

1 tablespoon olive oil
3 pounds skinless chicken, breasts and thighs
2 onions, sliced 1/4 inch slices
2 cups diced tomatoes
1 cup tomato sauce
2 cloves garlic, minced
1 1/2 teaspoon salt, or more
1/4 teaspoon pepper, or more
1/2 teaspoon celery seed
1/2 teaspoon sage
3 to 4 bay leaves

In a very large skillet, sauté onion slices in oil until soft and browned. Add remaining ingredients and then add chicken pieces, meat side down. Cover, reduce heat to simmer and cook for about 15 minutes. Remove cover and continue to cook for about 45 minutes. Turn meat often until very tender.

Serve over linguini.

CHICKEN PILAF
AKA "CHICKEN RICE AND RAISINS"

This is a recipe given to me by a friend. I made it often, as the boys loved it. When Justin and Matt were really young, they picked the raisins out. In time, they came to love the raisins as much as the chicken. It's been around our home for some 30 years now. Hopefully, you guys will make it for your own families, someday.

RECIPE

Preheat oven to 375F and grease a 2 quart casserole dish.

6 to 8 chicken pieces with the skin and bone. Do not use boneless
4 tablespoons butter
1 1/2 cups white rice
1/2 cup onions, chopped
2 cups water
4 tablespoons raisins
1/2 teaspoon salt
2 chicken bouillon cubes

In a large skillet, melt butter. Brown chicken pieces on both sides. Do not cook at this point, you just want to brown them. Sprinkle lightly with salt. Remove chicken from pan and set aside. In the same skillet drippings add in rice. Continue to cook the rice until it pops and is completely brown, 3-4 minutes. Add onion, bullion cubes and water. Bring to a boil and continue stirring until the bouillon is dissolved. Add salt and raisins last.

Pour rice mixture into prepared casserole dish. Top with chicken pieces, meat side down. Cover and bake for about 30-40 minutes, or until chicken is cooked through and rice has cooked completely. Chicken juices must run clear. Makes about 4 servings.

CHILE RELLENO

Preheat oven to 375F

3 7 oz cans whole green chilies
1 pound Monterey Jack cheese, grated
1 12 oz can evaporated milk, cold
1/2 cup flour
1 teaspoon salt
4 egg whites
1 8 oz can tomato sauce

Wash chilies, slice open up and lay flat
Using a 7x11x2 dish, line bottom with 1/2 of the chiles and spread
grated cheese over top. Place remaining chilies over cheese, fitting
closely together.

Whip egg whites until firm, but not stiff. The egg whites should form
soft peaks. Set aside.

Whip evaporate milk in a large bowl until it thickens, about 4 minutes.
Add salt and flour, mix well and fold in egg whites. Pour over chilies
and immediately place in pre heated oven. Bake for 40 minutes or
until golden brown. Remove from oven and carefully spread tomato
sauce on top. Bake for an additional 10 minutes. Let sit for about
15 minutes before trying to cut.

MOM'S HOMEMADE CHILI

What you'll need…

A very large dutch oven or pot
1 tablespoon oil
1 1/2 pounds ground beef
Chili powder, 2 teaspoons or as desired
Sugar, 1 tablespoon
Onion, 1 medium chopped
Green pepper, 1 medium chopped
2 pound can tomatoes (or 2 one pound cans) diced or crushed
1 lb can tomato sauce
Water, 1/2 cup
Garlic, 2 cloves crushed
Chili powder, 2 teaspoons or more if desired
Cumin, 2 teaspoons or to taste
1 small can Ortega diced green chilies
Red Pepper, dash
Red Kidney beans, 2 one pound cans, undrained. Any variety of
Spanish beans will work, including black beans
Salt and Pepper to taste

Using a heavy pot or dutch oven, heat oil until hot. Brown beef, sear
and crumble as it cooks. Sprinkle with chili powder, sugar, salt and
pepper to taste.

Meanwhile, chop onion and green pepper. Stir into seasoned beef
and cook until vegetables soften. Add tomatoes and tomato sauce
along with water, garlic, cumin, and can of chilies undrained.

Simmer for about 30 minutes. Add undrained beans and additional
chili powder, salt and pepper, if desired. Simmer uncovered for an
additional 30 minutes or longer, stirring occasionally.

Makes about 2 quarts or 6 servings.

CHINESE FRIED RICE

This dish brings me back to Camp Lajeune, North Carolina. Base housing. I remember standing at the stove next to mom, watching the rice fry and wanting to stir it myself. It had to fry for like 5 minutes, until the rice was popping and crisp. Mom told me that cooking the rice properly was the most important part of the recipe. It had to be fried hot enough or the rice would be sticky. She made it plain, but, later when I made it on my own, I added shrimp or beef. Carrots and other vegetables can be added as well.

RECIPE

4 cups, cooked and cold
3 tablespoons butter
2 eggs, slightly beaten
1 small onion, diced
3 cloves garlic, minced
3 green onions, thinly sliced
4 tablespoons soy sauce
1/2 teaspoon toasted sesame oil
Salt and pepper to taste

Cook rice til just tender. Refrigerate to cool

In a large saucepan, heat 1/2 tablespoon butter over high heat, add eggs and scramble. Remove eggs to a small bowl.

Melt 1 tablespoon butter in the same pan. Add onion, garlic and a pinch of salt and pepper.

Sauté for about 3 minutes until onions are tender. Increase heat to high and add in remaining 1/1/2 tablespoons butter.

Immediately add cold rice and green onions, soy sauce. Stir to combine. Fry in butter. Stirring occasionally, allowing rice to crisp in between, Roughly 4 minutes

Add eggs. Salt and pepper per taste. Add sesame oil and more soy sauce, if desired. Toss through rice. Serve immediately or refrigerate for up to 3 days.

CHOCOLATE OATMEAL BROWNIES

Preheat oven to 350F
Oil 9x13 baking pan

1/2 cup flour
1/2 teaspoon baking powder
1/4 teaspoon salt
1/2 teaspoon cinnamon
1/8 teaspoon nutmeg
1/2 cup butter, softened
1/3 cup brown sugar, packed
1/3 cup sugar
1 egg
1 teaspoon vanilla
1 cup old fashioned oats
1/2 cup chocolate chips

In a medium bowl, mix together flour, baking powder, salt, cinnamon and nutmeg. Set aside.

With an electric mixer, beat butter and sugars until light and creamy. Continue to beat in egg and vanilla. Batter should be light and fluffy.

Slowly blend the dry ingredients into the wet batter. Stir in oats and chocolate chips. Pour into prepared pan and bake for 20-25 minutes until lightly browned. Center should come out clean with a toothpick test. Cool completely before cutting.

CHOCOLATE RUM ROLL
WITH FUDGE SAUCE

Justin found this recipe in a magazine when he was about 12. He copied it himself. He was so excited to make it one Christmas. We had so much fun that first time we made it together, baking with love and making our own memories. Once it was finished, we agreed that it was really easy.

Although, it looks like you worked on it all day. Thank you, Justin

RECIPE

Preheat oven to 350F
Grease a 15x10x1 jellyroll pan, then line with wax paper

6 eggs, separated
1 cup sugar
4oz German Sweet Chocolate, melted
1/2 teaspoon rum extract
1 pint heavy whipping cream
Cocoa

Melt chocolate over hot water in a double boiler

In a large bowl, beat egg whites to a soft peak. Slowly add 1/2 cup sugar, 2 tablespoons at a time, until soft peaks form. In a separate bowl, beat egg yolks to a pale yellow color, roughly 8 minutes. Add remaining 1/2 up sugar, 1 tablespoon at a time, beating until very thick. Blend melted chocolate into egg yolks and then fold the mixture into the egg whites.

Spread in prepared pan. Bake 15 to 20 minutes, until the cake springs back when lightly touched. Cool cake until just slightly warm, about 15 minutes.

Whip the cream with rum extract until stiff. Set aside.
Sift cocoa over cooled cake until evenly covered. Remove cake from pan, cocoa side down, onto a separate sheet of wax paper. Then, peel the wax paper previously baked onto the bottom side the cake. Spread cream over cake and carefully, roll cake up along the long side.

Frost with the following fudge sauce

1 cup sugar1/2 cup heavy whipping cream
4oz unsweetened chocolate
1/2 cup buter
2 egg yolks, slightly beaten
1 teaspoon vanilla

Combine sugar and cream in a small saucepan over medium heat. Cook, stirring constantly until sugar dissolves and mixture just begins to boil. Add chocolate and butter, stirring until melted and smooth. Remove from heat and pour 1/4 cup chocolate into egg yolks very quickly. Pour egg yolks back into melted chocolate. Again, stir quickly. Over low heat, cook mixture about 3 minutes until sauce is shiny. Remove from heat and add vanilla. Makes 2 cups.

Frost cake roll with fudge sauce. Slice to serve.

CHOCOLATE WHIPPED CREAM FROSTING

Chill metal mixing bowl, beaters and cream for at least 15 minutes prior to mixing.

2 cups heavy whipping cream
1/4 cup unsweetened cocoa powder
1/2 cup powdered sugar

Add all ingredient to chilled bowl, and beat with an electric mixer for 4-5 minutes, or until still peaks form. (Scoop a spoonful and hold upside down. The cream should hold its shape.)

Use immediately. Any cream leftover can be put in a sealed container and refrigerated for up to 3 days.

CHOCOLATE ZUCCHINI NUT BREAD

This bread is another family recipe from Aunt Lois, mom's younger sister. They each loved growing a garden and eating what they grew. Whatever they didn't eat, was canned, frozen, baked or given away. We all know how zucchini takes over a garden, so every summer they both shared creative zucchini recipes.

This bread is very moist and will mold quickly if left out more than a day. It can be refrigerated for up to a week. It can also be frozen, if securely wrapped.

RECIPE

Preheat oven to 350F. No mention of greasing pans in the recipe. Based on past baking, I would grease and flour a bead pan.

3 1/2 oz semi sweet chocolate
3 eggs
1 cup oil
2 cups sugar
1 teaspoon vanilla
3 cups flour
1 teaspoon baking soda
1/4 teaspoon baking powder
1 teaspoon cinnamon
1 teaspoon salt
1 cup chopped walnuts

Combine all dry ingredients and set aside.

Melt chocolate over double boiler and water or carefully in a sauce pan. Let cool.

In a large bowl, beat eggs with an electric mixer until creamy. Add in oil, sugar, vanilla and chocolate. Mix well. With a wooden spoon mix in dry ingredients half at a time. Fold in nuts.

Pour into a standard loaf pan and bake for 1 hour or until center tests done.

CINNAMON ROLLS

Mom and Vernon would make these during the winter. One of the few times Vern baked with mom. I never had the opportunity to make these with mom, but I certainly ate them with her.

When I was searching through mom's cookbooks and papers, I found the original recipe with my brother's name on it. I wonder if Tim got this from school and brought it home to her.

RECIPE

Preheat oven to 375F. Grease a 9x13 pan. Flour a large surface to knead dough on. Grease a large bowl for dough to rise in.

1 package active dry yeast
1/4 cup water
3/4 cup scalded milk
1/3 cup shortening
1/4 cup sugar
1 teaspoon salt
2 eggs, beaten
1/2 teaspoon vanilla
3 1/2 cups unsifted all purpose flour.

1/4 cup melted butter
1/4 cup sugar
1/4 cup brown sugar
2 teaspoons cinnamon
1/4 cup chopped nuts (optional)
1/2 cup raisins (optional)

Dissolve yeast in water. Set aside.
Pour milk over shortening, sugar and salt. When shortening is completely melted, slowly add eggs and vanilla. Cool to lukewarm and stir in dissolved yeast. Mix well.

Gradually add only 3 cups flour, beating with wooden spoon until dough is smooth And too stiff to continue beating.

Turn onto a lightly floured surface and knead until smooth, about 8 minutes. Place dough in a well greased bowl. Cover with towel and let rise until the dough had doubled in size.

Turn onto very lightly floured surface and knead one minute.
Roll to about 17x12 rectangle. Spread roll with melted butter.

Mix together sugars and cinnamon. Spread evenly over dough. Sprinkle with nuts and raisins. Roll lengthwise and cut into 12 slices.

Place on prepared pan and bake about 20 minutes.

CINNAMON NUTS

This is an old recipe mom and I used to make during the Thanksgiving and Christmas holidays. You can use just about any nut. I always use walnuts, pecans and blanched almonds. Buying blanched almonds can be very expensive. So, mom and I blanched them ourselves. Trust me, it's a big process but spending all that time together was the silver lining. Mom and I would sit at the dining room table, her with a coffee and me with a glass of wine. We skinned each and every almond by hand.

We would take a 3 pound bag of raw almonds and put them into a very large pot of boiling water. Turn heat off and then allow them to sit for about 3-4 minutes. Then pour the hot nuts into a large colander. As the nuts are draining, the skins will start peeling off. That's the whole process. When nuts are completely dry, they're ready to roast.

Roast 3 cups nuts for about 15 minutes at 375F. However, when roasting the dried blanched almonds, roast them separately, as they may still be damp in the center. Almonds will pop when fully roasted. Stir often to prevent burning.

Make a syrup with following ingredients and butter a large cookie sheet or platter.

1 cup sugar
1/2 cup water
2 teaspoons (or more to taste) cinnamon
1 teaspoon salt
1 1/2 teaspoon vanilla

Place all but the vanilla into a medium size pot. Cook slowly over medium heat until the mixture reaches 235F on a candy thermometer, or until syrup forms a hard ball when dropped into a cup of cold water. This can take up to 10 minutes.

When ready, remove syrup from heat. With a wooden spoon, beat until the syrup looks creamy. Immediately add in vanilla, stirring as syrup bubbles and becomes creamy again. Pour syrup over roasted nuts and stir to coat completely. Turn onto the buttered platter and separate them as they cool.

It seems like a lot of work, but so worth it. They make a great gift for the holidays.

FRESH COCONUT CAKE

I believe that this cake, full of fresh coconut, was moms' all time favorite. Every time she made one she would remind me how our grandmother would bake this 5 layer desert from scratch, including the coconut she grated herself. Just cracking a coconut seems to be an event of its own.

Baking this cake brought back memories of moms childhood on the farm. Having all those mouths to feed kept her mother very busy. According to mom, our grandmother spent her entire day between their garden and the kitchen. Dawn to Dusk. And somehow this woman found time to grate a coconut? I'm so grateful we have the option to go to a box for the cake and bag for the coconut.

Here's the updated, user friendly recipe that mom used and it is great. There's a few favorite frosting recipes too. Plus, a surprise for Justin and Matt.

RECIPE

Preheat oven to 350F.

Grease and flour 3 cake pans

1 box yellow cake mix
1 small box (4 servings) instant vanilla pudding
1 1/3 cups water
4 eggs
1/4 cup oil
2 cups coconut
1 cup walnuts

Blend cake mix, pudding, water, eggs and oil. Beat with electric mixer on medium for 4 minutes. Stir in coconut and walnuts. Pour

into 3 prepared cake pans, evenly. Bake for 35 minutes or until center springs back when lightly touched.

Cool in pan for 15 minutes before removing to cooling rack.

COCONUT CREAM CHEESE FROSTING.

4 tablespoons butter (separated in half)
2 cups coconut (reserve 1/4 cup for top)
1 8 oz package of cream cheese (room temperature)
2 tablespoons milk
3 1/2 cups powdered sugar
1/2 teaspoon vanilla

Melt 2 tablespoons butter in skillet. Add coconut and stir until golden brown. Spread coconut on paper towel to cool. Cream the remaining 2 tablespoons butter with cream cheese. Add milk. Stir in powdered sugar and gradually blend in vanilla and then adding coconut. Spread on top of all 3 layers. Then spread around the sides. Sprinkle top with remaining coconut.

Note: Place the first layer of cake face down on a serving plate. After frosting add the 2nd layer face down on the frosting. Then the 3rd layer should be face up.

C 12   The Seattle Times   Wednesday, April 7, 1982

Delight the children with a whimsical, edible bunny, iced with fluffy coconut

What child wouldn't be delighted with this Easter Bunny Cake? It's a simple-to-fix cake, made from a mix and decorated with coconut and candy.

EASTER BUNNY CAKE
About 12 servings

1 box plain white cake mix
Seven Minute Frosting (recipe follows)
3 cups flaked coconut, divided
Red food coloring
1 red jelly bean
1 pink jelly bean
Black licorice laces
5 black licorice drops

1. Using the cake mix, bake two 9-inch round cakes, according to package directions. Cool.

2. Cut one cake as shown in diagram A. Cut the other cake as shown in diagram B, making the

TESTED RECIPES

largest square (6 inches) possible out of the round cake.

3. Arrange the square, for the body, and circle for the head on a serving tray, as shown in diagram C.

4. Stack 2 ring pieces from diagram A to form each paw; put 2 circular edges together, from diagram B, to make the ears. Prepare frosting and cover entire bunny.

5. Tint about ⅓ cup coconut with a few drops of red food coloring, until coconut turns pink. Decorate ears, nose and bottom paws with pink coconut. Next cover the rest of bunny all over with remaining white coconut.

6. Decorate mouth with red

jelly bean and nose with pink jelly bean.

7. Fashion whiskers, smiling mouth, bow tie and tiny toes out of black licorice laces.

8. Use 2 licorice drops for eyes and 3 for buttons on the body.

Seven Minute Frosting
Enough for Bunny Cake

2 egg whites (¼ cup)
1½ cups sugar
¼ teaspoon cream of tartar
⅓ cup water
1 teaspoon vanilla

1. Combine egg whites, sugar, cream of tartar and water in top of double boiler.

2. Place over boiling water and beat with a rotary beater until mixture stands in stiff peaks, about 7 minutes. Scrape bottom and sides of pan occasionally. Fold in vanilla. Use to frost bunny cake thickly.

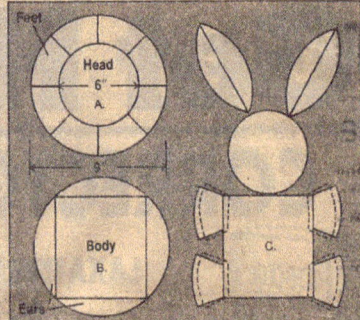

An Easter Bunny Cake doubles as a centerpiece and tasty dessert for the holiday.

FRESH COCONUT PIE

RECIPE FOR COCONUT PIE SHELL

Preheat oven to 450F

1/3 cup fresh coconut
1 1/2 cups sifted flour
1/2 teaspoon salt
1/2 cup butter
3 tablespoons cold water

Put the coconut into a blender. On low speed grate fine. Set aside. Mix flour and salt in medium bowl. Cut in butter with a pastry blender until the dough is crumbly or the size of small peas. Mix in the grated coconut. Sprinkle cold water, a tablespoon at a time and mix with a fork until the dough holds together. Shape into a ball. Roll out to fit a 10 inch pie pan. Crimp the edges and pierce the bottom with a fork. Chill for 30 minutes.

Bake for 12-15 minutes or until golden brown. Cool before filling.

COCONUT CHIFFON FILLING

1 1/2 tablespoons unflavored gelatin, (1 1/2 envelopes) with 1/4 cup water
3 tablespoons boiling water
4 eggs separated
1 teaspoon vanilla
1/4 teaspoon salt
3/4 cup sugar
1 cup fresh coconut

Soften gelatin in cold water and let stand in blender container until completely moistened. Add boiling water, cover and run on low speed until gelatin is completely dissolved. While still running the blender,

add egg yolks, one at a time. Stop blender. Add vanilla, salt and sugar. Cover and run on high speed until smooth.

Then add the coconut and cover again. Run on low speed until the coconut is finely grated. Chill in refrigerator just until mixture just begins to thicken.

While batter is chilling, beat egg whites in a medium bowl with an electric mixer until soft peaks form. Fold chilled gelatin mixture into beaten egg whites. Pour into pre baked pie shell.

Chill until firm. Top with sweetened whipped cream and grated coconut.

CORNBREAD SAUSAGE STUFFING
WITH APPLES

I found this recipe in the Seattle Times November 1985. We decided to try it. Fantastic. So, I made it with mom many Thanksgivings. This the only stuffing I've used since then. Mom still liked her giblets reduction the best, as that's what her momma made.

Best to read over the instructions prior to beginning, to be sure you have all the ingredients. The recipe calls for cornbread. I make mine the night before, or Thanksgiving eve.

12 tablespoons butter (1 1/2 sticks)
2 1/2 cups yellow onions, finely chopped
3 tart unpeeled apples, cored and cut into small chunks or cubes.
I prefer tarter apples, like Winesap or Johnathon. It's a preference as to the desired tartness.
1 pound bulk breakfast sausage with sage. Or any mild seasoned sausage. If bulk isn't available, mild Italian sausage links will work. Just remove the sausage from the casing before frying.
3 cups cornbread Crumble into coarse chunks
3 cups French read, crumbled into chunks
3 cups whole wheat bread crumbled into smatter chunks
2 teaspoons thyme
1 teaspoon kosher salt
1/2 spoon black pound pepper
1 teaspoon sage
1/2 cup Italian parsley, chopped
1 1/2 cups fresh pecans, quartered

In a large skillet, melt half the butter until bubbly. Add onions and sauté over medium heat until tender and lightly browned. About 25 minutes. Transfer to a very large mixing bowl and set aside.

In the same skillet, melt the remaining butter. Add the apple chunks, cover. Over high heat, cook until lightly brown, but not mushy. Transfer

apples and butter to mixing bowl with the onions. Using the same skillet, add in the sausage, crumble and cook over medium heat, stirring until lightly brown. Using a slotted spoon, transfer the sausage to the bowl with onion and apples, reserving the remaining fat.

Add in all other ingredients and combine gently. I mix this all together with my hands, being sure to wash them beforehand. Stuffing needs to cool completely before putting in the bird. If stuffing the turkey is not preferred, spooning the stuffing into a greased covered casserole dish will work perfectly fine, use what doesn't fit into the turkey. Just be sure to baste the stuffing, using same reserved fat. Bake at 325F for approximately 45 minutes.

MOM'S CORN CHOWDER

Corn chowder. Mom made it for us kids when money was tight. Yet, when I think of corn chowder, as an adult, it conjures up heavy cream, lots of butter and bacon. Those ingredients aren't included here. But what was included was a big heart full of love. "You can't buy love, it's given." So this recipe is just so mom. Not having money certainly didn't make any difference in the outcome. An addition of homemade biscuits can add a lot of smiles too. Most importantly, feel the love you have for those you might making it for.

RECIPE

1 small onion, chopped fine
2 tablespoon butter
2 cups boiled diced potatoes, just until tender (about 3 medium)
2 cups corn
1/2 teaspoon salt
2 cups hot or scalded milk
3 tablespoons flour
1/2 teaspoon celery salt
1/4 teaspoon pepper

In a large saucepan, sauté onion in butter. Add flour to butter and onions and mix well. Add milk slowly, to prevent lumping.

Add remaining ingredients and season to taste. Simmer over low heat for about 20 minutes.

CORNFLAKE CANDY

The story I got was that this was a concoction of mom's oldest sister, Ellen. The ongoing tale was that Aunt Ellen published her recipe in the cookbook of her local Baptist Church.

As mom shared the story, she and Aunt Lois decided to make the candy one Christmas. When it was finished, they sat down and ate a piece, immediately realizing something was missing in the recipe. The peanuts! Aunt Ellen had forgotten to mention the peanuts in the cookbook.

Here is the infamous recipe, including the peanuts.

Line a large rectangular cake pan with wax paper.
Butter the wax paper.
Also butter a large wooden spoon

In a very large bowl (or pot as mom did) mix together
7 cups Cornflakes
2 cups coconut
1 cup salted peanuts

Set aside.

In a large saucepan mix together
2 cups sugar
1 cup evaporated milk
1 cup dark Karo syrup

In a large saucepan, heat remaining ingredients over medium heat ad bring to a boil. Continue to boil until the temperature reaches 260F, on a candy thermometer.

If you don't have a candy thermometer, you can use a cup of very cold water. Just drop a small amount into the cold water. It should form a very hard ball and sink to the bottom,

Pour the hot mixture over the bowl of cornflakes. Quickly, using a large, buttered wooden spoon, stir until the candy has coated the dry ingredients completely. Immediately pour the mixture onto the buttered wax paper. With buttered and spoon, pack down lightly. Mom liked to butter her fingers to make this step easier.

Cool and cut into 2 inch squares.

CHRISTMAS GOOD FOR YOU
CRANBERRY BREAD

I found this recipe December 2000 while spending time with mom and Joe, about two weeks prior to her death. We thought it sounded really good. I definitely made this with love in my heart for mom. Though she wasn't eating much by then, she took a piece and loved it.

It's very moist and not too sweet. It makes a great gift for Christmas when baked in small bread tins. If you wrap them, be sure to give the breads away the same day you make it, or it may mold within a day or two. This is due to the moisture and wrapping. The recipe makes 1 regular loaf or 3 small loaves.

Preheat oven to 350F
Lightly coat the loaf pans with nonstick cooking spray.

RECIPE

1 cup all purpose flour
1/2 cup whole wheat four
1 cup sugar
1 1/2 teaspoon cinnamon
1/2 teaspoon salt
1/2 teaspoon baking soda

3 egg WHITES
1 cup applesauce
3 tablespoons buttermilk
1 1/2 cups fresh cranberries
1/2 cup chopped walnuts

In a medium bowl combine flours, sugar, cinnamon, salt and baking soda.

In a larger bowl, beat the egg whites at a high speed for 1 minute. Beat in applesauce and buttermilk. Gradually add the flour mixture and beat until just combined. Stir in cranberries and nuts.

Transfer mixture to the prepared loaf pan/pans. Bake for 45 minutes or until edges begin pulling away from the sides and a toothpick inserted into enter comes out clean. Smaller pans will take less time.

Cool for about 10 minutes before turning bread out from pan.

DATE NUT BREAD

I believe it was mom's sister, Lois, who shared this recipe with her. It's been part of our Christmas holiday for years. No idea why someone decided to use coffee cans. Maybe finding baking pans were difficult back then. But, these breads are made in 1 pound coffee tins. Mom drank Maxwell house coffee forever, so she saved the cans for making these breads.

After the breads are baked and cool, they're removed from the pans and stood up with the rounded crown on top. They'll resemble candles when finished.

Another side note. Do not double the recipe. A cardinal sin when baking with mom.

I made these last with Aunt Lois the weekend before mom died. Aunt Lois came to stay with mom for the weekend. Mom was just too sick to get up, though she tried. The baking needed to get done and time was running out. We needed to get Tim's annual package shipped in time for it to arrive before Christmas. So, my aunt and I did all the baking in those last 3 days.

As hard as it was on mom, she wanted to taste everything. We had no idea that would be our last weekend with her.

RECIPE

Preheat oven to 350F
Grease and flour 5 one pound coffee cans.

1 16oz package of pitted dates, chopped
1 teaspoon baking soda
2 cups water
2 cups sugar
2 eggs

2 tablespoons butter or vegetable oil
1/2 teaspoon salt
2 teaspoons vanilla.
4 cups self rising flour
1 1/2 cups walnuts

In a large saucepan place chopped dates and baking soda in water. Mix together and bring just to a boil. Set aside and let cool.

When mixture has cooled add butter and sugar. Then add eggs and stir until mixed well. Add salt and vanilla.

Lastly, add the flour 1 cup at a time and mix completely after each cup. Fill the prepared coffee cans 1/2 full.

Bake 45 minutes to an hour. Bread is done when a clean toothpick is inserted in the center of the bread and it comes out clean.

Remove from oven and let cool enough to handle. Carefully turn upside down and remove the bread. Immediately turn bread right side up and while still warm and glaze.

Glaze:
2 cups powdered sugar and just enough milk to make a medium paste. Add chopped maraschino cherries. Pour over each bread letting the glaze run down. Leave chopped cherries on top.

EVERYDAY LENTIL SOUP

2 tablespoons olive oil or avocado oil
2 cloves garlic, minced
2 small shallots, chopped
4 large carrots (thinly sliced, diagonally)
4 stalks celery (thinly sliced, diagonally)
1/4 teaspoon sea salt or kosher
1/4 teaspoon black pepper
3 cups baby red and/or yellow potatoes, chopped bite-size
4 cups vegetable broth (and more as needed). I like to use "Better than Bouillon" seasoned vegetable base and make my own broth. I can make it stronger and more flavorful.
2 sprigs fresh thyme or 1 teaspoon dried
1 smaller sprig fresh rosemary or 1/2 teaspoon dried.
1 cup uncooked green or brown lentils (rinsed and drained)
2 cups greens, optional (like collard greens or kale)

Heat large pot over medium heat. Once hot, add oil, garlic, shallots, carrots and celery. Season with with a bit of salt and pepper. Stir and sauté 4-5 minutes, until slightly tender and golden brown, being careful not to burn the garlic. Add more oil if necessary.

Add potatoes and season with more salt and pepper. Stir and cook for 2 minutes. Add vegetable broth, rosemary and thyme. Increase heat to medium high and bring to a rolling simmer. Add lentils and stir. Once simmering again, reduce heat to low and simmer uncovered for at least an hour. Check every 10 minutes or so to insure there is sufficient broth for the potatoes and lentils to cook thoroughly.

Usually, it's necessary to add more broth. It's a personal taste as to how thick you like the soup and how much seasoning you prefer. About 5 minutes before serving, add greens if desired. Cover and cook about 4 additional minutes. Uncover and let soup rest for 15 minutes after cooking.

MOM'S FRIED CHICKEN

Mom never had a recipe for fried chicken. She made it so often in her lifetime that the procedure became simply routine. For years, I watched her put 3 big scoops of Crisco into her old cast iron skillet and then I waited for it melt. The oil had to be spattering hot before she'd drop the chicken in it.

I remember that she placed the chicken in milk and then dredged the pieces into an egg mixture. She put the flour, salt and pepper into a paper bag. Then, she would put the chicken pieces, 2 at a time, in the bag and shake it. I loved doing that part.

That's it really. Except that she never left the chicken alone. She just kept standing there turning the pieces over and over. The crust would get really crispy and the golden brown. I think she may have put a lid over the thicker pieces for a few minutes. She used a fork to deeply prick the chicken and when the juices ran clear, she said they were done.

Once she felt the chicken was well done, she would placed them onto paper towels to drain. I think she may have had 3 to 4 pieces in he skillet at one time. So it took some time to get the whole chicken fried. So worth the effort. Crispy and juicy.

I'd like to say that I carried on this tradition of hers, but I didn't really like eating, nor cooking fried food. Explains why Justin and Matt spent so much time at Grandma's house.

FRIED CORNBREAD

Here's a staple in Country Cooking. Mom absolutely loved fried cornbread with a lot of butter. In one of our bonding moments, mom told me how our grandmother would fry up cornbread and the family would eat it with vegetables and eggs. Mom made it often, along with fried chicken, collard greens and fried okra. She thought fried cornbread went with everything. I liked watching her fry in that old cast iron skillet full of hot Crisco. That big spoon pushing the mixed cornmeal down in the bubbly oil.

RECIPE

1 cup flour
1 1/2 cup yellow cornmeal
2 tablespoons sugar
1 teaspoon salt
1 egg
3 tablespoons butter, melted
1 1/4 cup milk

Combine all dry ingredients, then whisk in milk, butter and egg. Stir well to combine. Batter should be slightly thick Add more salt or sugar, depending on taste.

In a cast iron skillet, melt 2 heaping tablespoons Crisco. Continue on high heat until oil spatters. Carefully add 2 heaping spoons of batter into the skillet and reduce heat to medium high. Pat down batter to about 1/2 inch thick. Continue to fry until sides begin to brown. Turn over and fry the other side. Unfortunately, there were no instructions as to how long to fry. I remember the interior was like cooked cornbread and the outside was crispy. I'm guessing 5 minutes per side.

This batter can be baked as well. Just add more sugar to equal 1/3 cup and add in 2 teaspoons baking powder. In the same caste iron skillet, melt 5 tablespoons butter. When butter is bubbling, pour batter into the skillet and bake at 400F for 18-20 minutes.

GERMAN STOLLEN

Unfortunately, mom and I didn't get an opportunity to make this together. Yet, I have never spent time kneading dough without thinking of her. She loved baking for us. I made so many desserts with her. Two things are important, she'd say, when baking. First, never double the recipe. Never. Second, bake with love in your heart during the entire process. Think of those special loved one who will be enjoying it.

This is one of my all time favorite holiday breads. I'm sure Justin and Matt remember waking up to this stollen on Christmas and Easter mornings. It's a lot of work for sure. I was known to spend many late hours in the kitchen, long after everyone went to bed. Thinking of the smiles in the morning were worth it.

The recipe makes 3 loaves. I usually ate most of it, not everyone liked candied fruit or fruit peels, yet that never deterred me. It's so festive and makes a lovely, thoughtful gift.

RECIPE

4 to 4 1/2 cups all purpose flour
1 package active dry yeast
1/4 teaspoon group cardamom
1 1/4 cups milk
1/2 cup butter
1/4 cup granulated sugar
1 teaspoon salt
1 egg, slightly beaten
1 cup raisins
1/4 cup chopped mixed candied fruits
1/2 cup dried currants
1/4 cup chopped blanched almonds
2 tablespoons finely shredded orange peel
2 tablespoons finely shredded lemon peel
1 cup powdered sugar, sifted

2 tablespoons hot water
1/2 teaspoon butter
Touch of lemon extract, if desired

In a large mixing bowl, combine 2 cups of the flour, yeast and carda-mom. Then, in a saucepan heat milk, 1/2 cup butter, sugar and salt until just warm and butter is almost melted, (115 to 120 degrees), stirring constantly. Add to flour mixture. Add egg and beat with an electric mixer on low speed for 1/2 minute, scraping sides of bowl constantly. Beat for 3 minutes on high speed. With a spoon, stir in as much of the remaining flour as you can mix. Stir in raisins, candied fruits and peels, currants and almonds.

Turn out onto a lightly floured surface. Knead in enough of the remain-ing flour to make a moderately soft dough that is smooth and elastic. About 3 to 5 minutes total. Shape into a ball and place in a greased bowl. Turn once, cover to let dough rise in a warm place until double, about 1 1/2 hours. When dough has risen, punch down and turn onto a lightly floured surface. Divide into thirds. Again, cover and let rest for 10 minutes.

Using a rolling pin, roll one section into a 10x16 rectangle. Without stretching, fold the long side over to within 1 inch of the opposite side. Press to seal. Place on prepared baking sheet. Then, repeat process with the remaining two sections. Once again, cover and let rise until nearly double, about 1 hour. Bake for 18 to 20 minutes until golden.

Combine powdered sugar, butter and hot water. Adding lemon extract, if desired. Brush over warm breads.

CHRISTMAS HEAVENLY CRESCENTS

We all remember these Christmas treats. Powdery and messy, but, really good with milk or coffee. These cookies go back to when mom lived on the farm.

RECIPE

Preheat oven to 325F. Line a cooke sheet with parchment paper

1 lb butter
6 tablespoons powdered sugar
6 tablespoons sugar
1 teaspoon vanilla
4 cups flour
1 lb pecans, ground fine. You can use walnuts as well.

Cream butter for 5 minutes with an electric mixer. Blend in both sugars and vanilla. Slowly, blend in flour and nuts. Roll into uniform size balls and place on prepared cookie sheet.

Bake for 20 minutes. When cool, roll in powdered sugar.

HERBED PORK LOIN CHOPS

1 teaspoon fresh sage
1 teaspoon fresh rosemary
2 medium garlic cloves, chopped
1 teaspoon salt and fresh ground pepper
4 center cut pork loin chops, at least an inch thick
2 tablespoons butter
1 tablespoon peanut oil
3/4 cup dry white wine

Combine sage, rosemary, garlic, salt & pepper and chop together to create a very fine paste. Spread and press herb paste firmly on both side of chops.

Melt butter and oil in heavy 12" skillet for about a minute or two to heat up. Brown chops on both sides, turning once with tongs. Remove chops from pan and drain all but a small amount of fat. Add 1/2 cup wine and bring to a full boil. Return chops to pan, cover and reduce heat. Simmer on low heat about 25 minutes. Remove chops again. Add remaining wine to skillet and boil down to a syrupy glaze. Drizzle on chops prior to serving.

ITALIAN LENTIL SOUP

1 tablespoon olive oil
1/3 cup chopped onion, 1 small
1/3 cup chopped celery 1 stalk
1 cup thinly chopped, diagonally. About 2 medium
5 cups water
4 cups cabbage cut into 1 inch pieces, about 1/2 head
1 cup uncooked lintels, rinsed and drained
1 cup tomato puree
1 1/2 teaspoons sugar
1/2 teaspoon crushed dried oregano
1 bay leaf
1 teaspoon salt
1/4 teaspoon pepper

Heat oil in a dutch oven or large pot. Add onion, celery and carrots. Sauté until vegetables are slightly tender. Stir in water, cabbage, lentils and remaining ingredients. Bring to a boil and reduce heat. Cover and simmer for 45 minutes or longer until the lentils are very soft. It may be necessary to add more water to prevent the soup from becoming too thick.

Makes 5 servings

JUSTIN'S CHOCOLATE COOKIES

When Justin was probably 8 years old, grandma Rita noticed how much he liked baking with me. So, that year, she bought him his own cookie cookbook for his birthday. Out of all the cookie recipes, this is the one he wanted to bake. I'm sure Justin remembers baking these with grandma. With a little assistance, he made them by himself. Or at least the mixing part. Grandma loved to give him the spoon and and beaters to lick. That was most likely Justin's favorite part, other than maybe spooning the dough on to the cookie sheet.

RECIPE

Preheat oven to 300F
Lightly grease a cookie sheet

16 squares Bakers Chocolate, guessing semi sweet
3/4 cup brown sugar
1/4 cup butter
2 eggs, slightly beaten
1 teaspoon vanilla
1/2 cup flour
1/4 teaspoon baking powder

From this handwritten copy of the recipe, I can see that most of the directions were in Grandma's head. I'm just filling in the "how to" part based on similar recipes.

Melt the remaining solid chocolate with the butter on low heat. Maybe using a double boiler over water, as chocolate burns quickly. Once melted, remove from heat and add brown sugar, vanilla and eggs. Stir quickly as not to cook the eggs.

Stir together the flour and baking powder together. Then stir in the flour mixture and chopped chocolate.

Drop by heaping teaspoons onto prepared cookie sheet. Bake for 8 to 10 minutes, being careful not to over bake or they will be hard after cooling.

LIME JELLO DESSERT
WITH CHOCOLATE COOKIE CRUST

Such a wonderfully light dessert during the summer or after a heavy meal. It's fun to make and everyone likes it.

1 box "Famous Chocolate Wafers". (Found in the cookie aisle)
1 tablespoon butter, melted
1 14.5oz can evaporated milk, cold
1 cup sugar
1 3 oz box of Lime gelatin
1/4 cup lime juice

Chill evaporated milk in freezer for at least 1.5 hours.

Boil 1 cup water. In a large mixing bowl, add jello mix and stir until completely dissolved. May take a couple of minutes. Fill a measuring cup with 1 cup ice cubes. Then add water to the 3/4 cup level. Pour liquid into the jello. Stir until it starts to thicken and ice cubes melt. Allow to set until the mixture looks like the consistency of a yogurt or mayo.

While jello is setting, use a rolling pin to crush the cookies. Or you can put cookies in a bag and roll over them to crumble. Add melted butter and mix well. Take half the mixture and pat down in a 9x13 pan. Save remaining mixture.

When jello has thickened enough, whip with an electric mixer until light and fluffy. May take a few minutes. Slowly add sugar and lime juice. Continue mixing until blended. Set aside.

Remove evaporated milk from freezer. In a separate mixing bowl, beat milk until stiff peaks form. Gently fold jello mixture into the whipped milk until uniform in color.

Pour mixture over cookie crust. Gently sprinkle remaining 1/2 cookie mixture on top. Refrigerate for at least an hour.

MAPLE NUT TWIST

This recipe was used so much, I had a tough time deciphering it. Mom and Vern used to make this together on Saturday mornings, probably, because it takes two to knead the bread. I never made it myself, but I ate plenty. Looks like a lot of work. Well worth the effort, though.

RECIPE

Preheat oven to 400F. Grease a large bowl, including sides, as well as a large cookie sheet.

4 1/2 to 5 cups flour
2 packages instant dry yeast
1/4 cup brown sugar
1 teaspoon salt
1/2 cup milk
1/2 cup water
1/4 cup maple syrup
1/4 cup butter or margarine
2 eggs slightly beaten
3/4 cup chopped walnuts

In a large mixing bowl, combine 2 cups of the flour, yeast, sugar and salt. Mix well and set aside.

In a saucepan, warm milk, water, syrup and butter to about 125 degrees. Butter does not have to melt completely. Add this wet mixture to flour mixture and blend on low speed of an electric mixer until moistened. Add in eggs and beat on medium speed for 3 minutes. Fold in walnuts by hand and enough remaining flour to make a firm dough.

Pour out onto a floured surface and knead until smooth and elastic, about 5 minutes. Place dough in the prepared bowl and turn to grease

the entire surface. Cover with a clean kitchen towel and let rise in a warm place for about an hour. Dough should double in size. (Mom would put the dough Inside a slightly warm oven, or over the dryer to rise.) When dough has risen enough, punch down and divide into 3 equal parts. On a floured surface, roll each part to make a 15" strand. Then just loosely braid the three rolls together. Pinch the ends of the braid and tuck under to seal.

Place the braid on prepared cookie sheet and cover again and let rise. Place in a warm place, about 30 minutes. Dough should be light and double in size again.

Bake for 25-30 minutes until golden brown. Remove from oven and let cool. Glaze using the following recipe.

Combine 1 cup powdered sugar, 1/4 teaspoon maple flavoring and 2 to 3 tablespoons milk. Blend until smooth and a little on the thicker side. Pour over the bread.

MOLASSES SUGAR COOKIES

Traditionally, Mom baked these cookies twice a year. Christmas and May 19th, Tim's birthday. She knew how much he loved them. Each time mom and I made them, she would remind me how my brother ate them by the dozen. (Explains why we made so many.)

We would sit for hours rolling the dough into little balls, then rolling them in sugar. As we rolled, she'd continue to impress the importance of keeping the balls uniform in size. This insured the cookies would be uniform. As with everything mom baked, she did it with pride.

The night that mom passed, we all went back to the house and on the table was "the box". Tim's Christmas box, full of cookies and beef jerky. My brother sat down, right there, and ate all 4 dozen cookies packaged for him. Tears rolling down his cheeks didn't slow him down.

In retrospect, I realize that the hours spent with mom at the table were much more than just making cookies. We talked and laughed and even cried at times, as we grew closer. If you have someone to bake these with, you might want to utilize the time for a little bonding.

RECIPE

3/4 cup shortening, like Crisco, or butter.
1 cup white sugar
1/4 molasses
1 egg

2 cups white flour
2 teaspoon baking soda
1/2 teaspoon salt
1/2 teaspoon ground cloves
1/2 teaspoon dry ginger

Preheat oven to 350 degrees

Melt shortening in large saucepan and let cool until just warm. Add sugar, molasses and egg. Whisk together until completely blended and thickened.

In a separate bowl sift together remaining dry ingredients. Add flour mixture to wet mixture and blend well. Mixture will be a thick dough.

Refrigerate the dough in clear wrap until it is set enough to form the balls. Roughly 20 minutes.

Pinch off a small amount of dough and in the palm of your hand, roll the dough into small balls. Try to keep them similar in size. Roll them into a bowl of white sugar to coat them.

Bake on dry cookie sheet about 8-9 minutes. Do not over bake, unless you prefer them crispy. Remove quickly.

Store in covered container to prevent drying. If they become too hard add a piece of bread to the container and reseal.

NANAIMO BARS
FROM NANNY

This had to be Nanny's favorite of her British holiday treats. Justin, I know you remember sneaking pieces every time she brought them for Christmas dinner. She eventually gave the recipe to me so I could make them for you. So, Justin, this one's for you.

Butter a 9 x 13 pan

1/2 cup butter
1/4 cup sugar
3 tablespoons cocoa
1 egg, slightly beaten
1 teaspoon vanilla
2 cups graham cracker crumbs
1 cup finely chopped coconut
1/2 cup walnuts

In a double boiler over hot water melt butter, sugar cocoa, egg and vanilla. Remove from heat and add graham cracker crumbs, coconut and walnuts. Spread mixture in a buttered pan.

Cover crust with the following:

1/4 cup softened butter
2 cups powdered sugar
3 tablespoon "POWDERED VANILLA CUSTARD MIX". Canadian or English works. Check your British specialty shops.
3 tablespoons milk

Combine ingredients and cover graham cracker crust. Refrigerate to chill.

Top custard layer with the following:

4 squares chocolate: 2 squares semi-sweet, 2 squares bittersweet.
1 tablespoon butter

Met chocolate over low heat, being careful not to burn. You can melt it in a double boiler over high heat as well.

Pour melted chocolate over custard layer and refrigerate until chocolate topping sets. Cut into small squares

SCOTTISH OAT SCONES
BY NANNY

This is a favorite Brealey recipe. Justin and Matt, I'm sure you remember these. Delicious warm with lots of butter and tea.

RECIPE

Preheat oven to 400F
Lightly grease a cookie sheet
Lightly flour a rolling surface

1 1/2 cups flour
1 cup uncooked oats
1/4 cup granulated sugar
1 tablespoon baking powder
1/4 pound butter, (1/2 cup or 1 stick)
1/2 cup raisins
1/3 cup milk
1 egg, slightly beaten
1tablespoon sugar combined with 1/8 teaspoon cinnamon

In a large mixing bowl, combine flour, oats, sugar and baking powder. Mix well and cut butter in until mixture is crumbly. This can be done with slicing two knives together or a handheld pastry knife. Stir in raisins

In a separate bowl combine milk and egg. Using a fork, mix together until the dough is moist. Turn onto floured surface and knead 8 to 10 times. Roll into a circle about 1/2 inch thick. Sprinkle with remaining sugar and cinnamon.

Cut into wedges and place on prepared cookie sheet. Bake for about 12-15 minutes, or until lightly browned.

PANKO TURKEY CUTLETS

1.5 pounds turkey cutlets about 4 cutlets
1 cup flour
1/2 teaspoon salt
1 teaspoon poultry seasoning
1 teaspoon black pepper
1 egg
2 tablespoon water
1 cup Panko bread crumbs
2 tablespoons butter
3 tablespoons olive oil

Preheat the oven to 350F

In a large bowl or plate, mix the flour, salt, pepper and seasonings.

In a second bowl, beat egg and water. Set aside.

In a third large bowl or plate, mix the Panko and parmesan cheese.

Bread turkey in this order: egg, flour, egg, Panko. Pressing the flour and bread crumbs on really well. Set turkey aside while you heat the skillet.

In a large cast iron or heavy skillet, heat butter and oil over medium heat until the butter is totally melted and bubbling. Add breaded turkey (about two cutlets at a time) and cook 3-4 minutes per side until just golden.

Transfer to a cookie sheet and cook the remaining two.

When all are browned, transfer cutlets to the oven and bake about 10 minutes. If your cutlets are thin (less than 1/2 inch) you may be able to cook them through on the stove top without putting them in the oven. Internal temperature should reach 160F when done. Serve warm.

Garden Fresh · **Every Time**

VICTORIA'S CANNERY

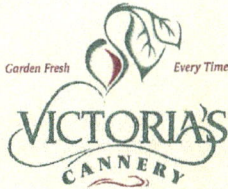

Fresh, Delicious, Natural Foods

NEW! PICKLED VEGETABLES
The perfect complement to grilled salmon – tangy, tasty pickled vegetables.

A delightfully light appetizer or accompaniment to SeaBear Salmon, Hogue Farms Pickled Asparagus, and Oh 'Brine's Garlic Mushrooms are made in Prosser, Washington. Victoria's Cannery Spicy Pickled Beets created by a mother and daughter duo from Kirkland, Washington.
M1026 Three 12 oz. jars **$19.95**

Getting back to our roots...

The inspiration for "Victoria's Cannery" came about when my mother began canning pickled beets, just like Grandma used to make. The "fresh from the garden taste" was so good, I ate them straight from the jar. As we shared them with friends, the demands for more came pouring in.

While digging into our roots, we discovered that the age old recipe for our pickled beets was handed down from my great-grandmother, a North Carolina Cherokee Indian, to my grandmother, Victoria.

With 13 children to feed, Grandma Victoria's life was spent cooking and canning. She took pride in making certain that her fruits and vegetables were cooked to perfection. Each jar was packed with care. To Grandma, appearance was just as important as taste.

The same is true today at Victoria's Cannery, Inc. Before leaving our kitchen, every jar is inspected to ensure that taste, texture and appearance are of superior quality.

We're proud of our Southern roots and are honored to share the recipes that represent our heritage.

So, Grandma Vic, we dedicate Victoria's Cannery to you. Your spirit lives on.

Our products are made with the principles of "care, pride, and excellence" that we inherited from our ancestors.

We stand by every jar. If for any reason you are not completely satisfied, please call us at 1-800-603-1323.

Rita Bruce
daughter

Pamela Brealey
grandmother

AND THE BEET GOES ON...
Victoria's Cannery Pickled Beets have been our traditional favorite for years.

Historically, the red beet, a rich colored vegetable root, was first discovered in Northern Africa.

For centuries, both England and Germany found this wonderful garden produce a welcomed and healthy addition to their dinner tables. But it was not until the 19th century, when the first sugar beet factory opened in Poland, that Americans first began to cultivate the beet.

Beyond their delicious taste and beautiful appearance, Victoria's pickled beets are highly nutritious and an excellent source of folate in natural occurring B Vitamin and Potassium.

We know you'll enjoy Victoria's Cannery Pickled Beets as much as we do.

Garden Fresh · **Every Time**

VICTORIA'S CANNERY

Pickled Beets

NET WT. 16 OZ. (1 LB.)
KIRKLAND, WA 98033

100% NATURAL, NO ADDITIVES

Nutrition Facts

REFRIGERATE AFTER OPENING.

Victoria's Cannery, Inc. 13 Central Way Suite 207   Kirkland, WA 98033 **206.603.0464** fax 206.603.0494

PICKLED BEETS

I really can't describe the significance of Mom's pickled beets. For as long as I can remember, every early summer she would start canning beets.

Being born and raised on a tobacco farm in Kinston, North Carolina, she learned quite young all about gardening and storing food for winter. She learned to can most anything, peaches, vegetables, pickles, jam, you name it, she canned it. Beets were one of her favorite foods. She ate them right out of the jar.

Every year, mom would make dozens of jars of these pickled beets. And, then, give most of them away to colleagues, friends and neighbors. These pickled beets became so popular that she had standing orders for her annual batch.

On a Spring day in 1996, I sat in mom's dining room watching her put lids on all these hot jars. I jokingly suggested that she start a beet business. My thought was, at least, she could recoup some of her expenses. But, as expected, she laughed and told me that she couldn't imagine selling them. Making the beets was a joyful pastime and she was happy giving them away.

That summer, I decided to research the idea of making pickled beets a real business venture. I found a somewhat local cannery in the small town of Gold Bar, WA. I couldn't believe that they rented their canning operations to smaller, independent wholesalers. We could contract out the entire canning process, including labor. We only needed to supply the ingredients and mom's specifications. They could be bottled in pint size jars, or gallon size cans and shipped anywhere.

After some crazy negotiating and some start up capital (Thank you, Brealey Ins), the vision was becoming a reality. Mom wanted to name the company "Victoria's Cannery". After her mother and my grandmother. We then got a business license and made it official.

Joe was able to help out with our "beet" logo, by finding the perfect graphic designer in LA. We were on our way! In retrospect, I realize the reason for creating this business wasn't about the beet, but the cooking. Much like the well known Arthur Ashe quote "It's the journey that's most important, not the destination". Mom and I had so much fun deciding on jars, lids, fabric and ribbon for the bonnet.

All the spices were bought in bulk and shipped to the cannery along hundreds of pounds of farmed beets. Mom arrived on the production floor with her own recipe and specific instructions on cooking and cutting the beets. To be clear, she inspected every step of the way to getting those pickled beets into hot, sterilized jars. Occasionally, driving the staff crazy. If she was putting her reputation on the line, those beet were damned well going to be made perfectly, she'd see to it. And, that, she did. Every batch that got made in that cannery, was inspected and tasted, usually by mom. That meant that we would have to be on the scene most days for some long hours. Sometimes, it was so cold and damp in that building that our fingers would go numb. We'd stand at the cutting area and hold the warm beets to let our hands thaw out.

After long hours, we would sometimes get silly. Something would strike us as goofy and it would start. One of us would get the giggles, and then the other would start. Bringing us both bent over in laughter, until one of us had to pee. Which, of course, would make us laugh even harder.

We lived on coffee and beets. In mom's case, it was coffee, beets and cigarettes. The work was physical and sometimes difficult for mom. But she was so excited to see everything coming together, it was all worth it.

By fall, we were selling them in local specialty stores. Trying to market them wasn't really all that difficult. After meeting with several smaller chains, we were able to sell them by the jar as well as to some deli's. "Made in Washington" stores featured our company in their monthly magazine. We were then able to ship the to "Mother's Markets" in Southern California.

Things were looking great, until they weren't. It was the fall of 1997 when I was diagnosed with vocal cord cancer. Unable to speak for almost 7 months, the business portion of the work fell on moms' shoulders. Unfortunately, during that same time period, she became ill, herself. Experiencing severe fatigue and back pain. Her diagnoses came early spring the following year. Stage 4 lung cancer. We were all devastated.

With that news, we were forced to liquidate Victoria's Cannery and in full circle, gave all remaining jars to everyone we knew. Only this time around, the jars were beautifully dressed. Red bonnets tied with green ribbons holding a small card describing the history of Victoria's Pickled Beets. Mom and I wrote the message and then each signed it.

We were both so proud of our accomplishment! Even though we were unable to bring the company to its fruition, we felt it was truly a successful venture. Not only did we learn and grow professionally, but, we gained understanding and respect for each other. Blessed with a window of time in which we were more than mother and daughter, we were partners.

Not only have I provided this recipe for those of you willing to take on the challenge of canning, but, I've provided pictures and information on Victoria's Cannery.

RECIPE

The one minor problem in mom's handwritten recipe is that mom didn't mention how many beets you'll need. I would start with about 3 pounds beets with stems still on.

You'll need about 8 pint size jars with seals and lids or with self sealing lids. The easiest way to get them hot enough and sanitized, is to use your dishwasher. Start with a clean, empty dishwasher and place all jars upside down on racks along with the lids. Turn on power wash and heat dry. While jars are being dried, prepare beets and syrup. If the jars dry before you're ready to fill them, set dishwasher to dry cycle and turn back on. This will ensure that they stay hot.

Cover whole beets with water and cook about 15 minutes, or until tender but not too soft. It's vital that the beets are not overcooked. According to the VP Operations, beets should never be mushy. Prick with a sharp knife to test for doneness. Remove from heat and drain. Immediately plunge into ice cold water. When cool enough to handle, remove skins and let completely cool down.

When cool, cut into quarters and then quarter again.

In a large pot, make syrup by bringing the following ingredients to a boil:

2 cups water
2 cups sugar
2 cups vinegar
1 teaspoon whole cloves
1 teaspoon
1 teaspoon cinnamon

Add cut beets to syrup and simmer for 15 minutes. Do not bring to a boil.

Then remove the hot jars from dishwasher and pack them with cut beets. Using a large ladle, cover beets with syrup to top of jar. There will be whole cloves left at the bottom of the syrup. Spoon some into each jar. Then, put lids on the jars, seal tightly. As they cool, the seal will pop down.

Mom and I also sold these beets with onions. Just place thinly sliced onions in jars before adding the beets. Thinly sliced lemons can also be added. Although, we never used lemons.

FLAKY PIE CRUST

Moms recipe out of an old Bon Appetite magazine. She thought it was the best

RECIPE FOR 2 PIE CRUSTS

1 1/4 cup all purpose flour. Plus a little extra on hand for rolling the dough.
1/2 teaspoon salt
1/2 teaspoon sugar
1 8 oz stick of butter (cold). Cut in squares
2 Tablespoons ice water

In a large food processor combine flour, salt and sugar. Pulse to combine.

While running the processor on medium speed, put in butter, a few squares at a time. Continue until the dough has become crumbly. Add water slowly, one tablespoon at a time. Process until the dough balls up.

Turn out onto a floured surface and divide in half. Roll each into ball and cover with Saran wrap. Chill until the dough is firm again.

Remove from refrigerator and place on a floured surface. Working one crust at a time, flatten the dough into a round 6" disc. Turn the disc over. Flour your rolling pin and sprinkle a very small amount on this side of the dough.

Begin rolling the dough from center out around the circle of the disc. To be sure it is large enough, take your pie plate and set it on the rolled dough. Continue rolling from center out to desired size.

Flour rolling pin again and slowly roll the dough onto the pin. Place the rolled up dough over the pie plate one side first. Then just unroll the dough onto the pie plate.

Pat the dough down and roll up all sides to make the crust. When sides are rolled up along the top of the pie plate, take both index fingers and press together to form grooves in the dough. Continue around the pie plate. This secures the crust and gives the pie a pretty finish.

NANNY'S
POPOVER CHICKEN

Another Brealey recipe loved by all. Justin and Matt, I decided to leave this recipe in this revised edition as it's not quite as involved as her popovers. It's a delicious British recipe, great for dinner.

2 1/2 to 3 pound fryer chicken cut into pieces
2 tablespoons cooking oil
Salt and Pepper
3 eggs
1 1/2 cups milk
1 tablespoon cooking oil
1 1/2 cups flour
3/4 teaspoon crushed dried tarragon leaves
1/2 teaspoon salt

In a large 2 in skillet, over medium heat brown chicken in hot oil. Turn often to prevent burning. Salt and pepper as desired.

Place browned chicken in a well greased 13x9x2 baking dish.

In a mixing bowl, beat eggs, milk and oil together. In a separate bowl, stir flour, tarragon and salt. Add flour to egg mixture. Beat with an electric mixer until completely smooth.

Pour egg batter over chicken and bake at 350F for about 50-60 minutes or until chicken is done.

MOM'S PORK ROAST WITH HOMEMADE APPLESAUCE

This was one of Joe's favorite dinners. Whenever he was in Seattle for a visit mom did her best to make it for him, along with mashed potatoes, steamed string beans and homemade biscuits. Always adding a special dessert. And, you can bet she was feeling love for Joe as she was cooking.

Mom was very particular in selecting a pork roast. She only bought the loins with he bone on. (Be sure to have the backbone cut and loosened for easy carving). It should be somewhat lean and pink. She'd figure about a half pound for each person. Which is ridiculous unless you're a wrestler. Usually a quarter pound is sufficient. Mom had issues about the amount of food she put on the table. She never wanted to run out of food.

RECIPE: Preheat oven to 325F

1 teaspoon salt
1/2 teaspoon pepper
1 teaspoon ground sage
1/2 teaspoon dried thyme

Combine all ingredients in a small bowl. You'll need a small roasting pan, size depending on the size of the roast. Never roast in a pan too large for the roast, as the drippings will burn. You will want the drippings for gravy.

Place roast fat side up in pan. Rub seasonings over the top and sides of the roast. Bake until the interior center of the pork registers 185F. Figure about 35 min per pound depending how done you like it. Remove roast from oven and let stand 10 minutes. Remove from pan and cover with foil while making the gravy in the roasting pan, using the drippings. (See gravy recipe)

While roast is baking, peel and core about 8 apples. Mom liked Granny and Fiji for their firmness. Cut apples into 1/2 inch slices and place in a large pot with about 1/2 cup sugar, 1/2 teaspoon cinnamon and a dash of nutmeg. Stir to coat apples, then add 1 teaspoon butter, cover and cook slowly over low heat. As apples steam, they will slowly soften. Cook until desired tenderness is reached. Let cool and thicken before serving.

RAW APPLE CAKE

Mom loved to bake about as much as she loved talking with her family. With mom being second to the youngest of thirteen children, many of her nieces and nephews were her age or even older. As was the case with mom and Linda. Linda was the daughter of moms older sister, but they're the same age. They both loved to share recipes whenever they chatted on the phone, which, according to mom, was never enough. Linda still lived in North Carolina and we know mom was now in Seattle. This is one of those recipes mom wrote down as they were talking.

RECIPE

Preheat oven to 350F
I'm assuming you need to grease and flour the 13x9 cake pan.

4 diced apples. Your choice I guess.
2 eggs
1/2 cup oil
2 cups sugar
3/4 teaspoon salt
1 1/2 teaspoon cinnamon
3/4 teaspoon nutmeg
2 cups flour
1 teaspoon baking soda
1 cup of nuts. I'd go with walnuts, but your choice here.

In a large bowl, break eggs over apples, add oil and mix well. Stir in the sugar and salt. Set aside.

In a smaller bowl add flour, cinnamon, nutmeg and baking soda. Add flour mixture too apples and mix well to coat. Fold in the nuts.

Pour into prepared pan and bake for 45 minutes to an hour, or until the center tests done.

OLD FASHIONED RICE PUDDING

One thing we all learned growing up with mom was how she never, ever wasted food. From many of the stories she told me about living on the farm with her siblings, it was clear that they were really "dirt poor" and often there was little food to go around. So when she began her own cooking, she tried her best to use everything. As with any rice leftover, she'd use it in pudding. "There were so many children without food, it was a sin to throw anything away."

RECIPE

Preheat oven to 350F
Butter a 1 1/2 quart baking dish.

Mix together:

2 eggs (slightly beaten)
2 cups milk
3/4 cup sugar
1/4 teaspoon salt
1 teaspoon vanilla
1/2 cups raisins
1/4 teaspoon nutmeg
1/4 teaspoon cinnamon
2 1/2 cups cooked white rice

Pour mixture into prepared baking dish. Set the dish into a larger pan filled with 1 1/2 inches hot water. Bake for about an hour. Pudding will be partially set when removed from oven.

Let cool and continue setting.

SEASONED ROASTED POTATOES

2 1/2 pounds red small potatoes, quartered
1/4 cup olive oil
415 teaspoons garlic powder
2 teaspoons thyme, crushed
Paprika and parsley
Salt and pepper

Preheat oven to 375F

In a large pot, add quartered potatoes and add enough water to cover the potatoes. Bring to a boil and immediately reduce heat to medium and continue to cook for only 5 minutes. Drain.

Combine oil and seasonings in a large bowl. Place hot potatoes in oil mixture and coat well. Arrange potatoes in a single layer on a baking pan. Any oil mixture left in the bowl can be drizzled over potatoes prior to baking. As the potatoes have already been precooked, bake for for about 30 minutes or until they are tender and golden brown. You can place under broiler for a few minutes to add more crispness.

This recipe can also be used with raw potatoes. The baking time needs to be increased to about 1 hour.

ROCKY ROAD CANDY

Never a Christmas went by without mom making this traditional fudge. The only variation may have been colored marshmallows and rolling the chocolate. It was to resemble stained glass windows. Later when I went on to make my own Christmas memories with Justin and Matt, I discovered another recipe that I liked better. From then on mom and I shared both kinds

MOM'S RECIPE FIRST

Lightly grease an 8 inch square pan.

12 oz chocolate chips
1/2 cup butter or margarine
2 cups sugar
1 cup miniature marshmallows
2/3 cups evaporated milk
1 teaspoon vanilla
1 cup walnuts
1/2 cup miniature marshmallows, frozen

Place chocolate chips and butter in a large bowl. Set aside.

In a heavy saucepan combine sugar, 1 cup unfrozen marshmallows and milk. Bring to a boil over medium heat and boil for 5 minutes, stirring constantly. Pour hot mixture over chocolate chips and butter. Blend until mixture begins to thicken. Stir in vanilla, walnuts and frozen marshmallows. Pour into prepared pan. Chill until firm before cutting. To make the round stained glass windows, use colored marshmallows. Turn chocolate onto buttered wax or parchment paper and roll immediately into a round log. Refrigerate until firm. Cut long into 1/2 inch slices.

PAM'S VERSION

Line a 13x9 cookie sheet with wax paper.

1 (12oz) package of chocolate chips
1 (12 oz) can come condensed milk
2 tablespoons butter
1 (12 oz) jar dry roasted peanuts
1 (10 1/2 oz) package miniature marshmallows
*Paraffin wax if desired

In a large bowl mix peanuts and marshmallows. Set aside.

Using the bottom pot of a double boiler, heat 1 cup water over medium heat. In the upper pot, pour milk and chocolate chips then melt over hot water, stirring constantly.

Pour chocolate mixture over marshmallows and peanuts. Quickly but gently fold together, stirring just enough to coat them with chocolate. Turn onto prepared cookie sheet. Chill completely and cut into squares.

*Paraffin is used in chocolate to provide a nice shine. 1/2 teaspoon can be added to the chocolate and milk and then melted together.

ROSETTES

Justin and Matt, I know you remember these little cookies. Snowflakes, stars and hearts, deep fried thin as tissue paper and covered in powdered sugar. You couldn't eat one without wearing all that powdered sugar. I made them every Christmas when you two were growing up, without exception. You both wanted to help put the battered iron into the hot oil. Of course, that never happened. I made you wait until the cookies were finished cooking and out on paper towels. Then you got to sift the powdered sugar all over them.

These rosettes are for sure a family tradition. It's my hope that you will make them for your own children and pass down the fun.

Before you start, you'll need the rosette iron forms and the handle to hold the irons. These should be available at any kitchen specialty store. I still have moms ancient set. It's so old that the threads barely hold the iron forms anymore. Yet, I still managed to use them last year.

RECIPE

Makes about 6 dozen cookies

Put enough Crisco or high temperature oil in a deep fat fryer or large dutch oven to fill 2/3 full. Heat to 400F. Have plenty of paper towels or paper bags lined up ready to place the cookies on when you take them out of the oil.

Please wear oven mitts while frying.

2 eggs slightly beaten
2 teaspoons sugar
1 cup milk
1 teaspoon salt
1 cup all purpose flour
1 tablespoon lemon extract

With an electric mixer, beat egg and sugar together. Add milk and mix well. In a separate bowl, mix together the flour and salt. Add to egg mixture and beat until very smooth. Batter would be the consistency of heavy cream. Beat in the lemon extract.

The rosette forms must be heated thoroughly before dipping them in the batter. Dip the forms into the hot oil for about 30 seconds. Drain the forms on paper towels to remove excess oil. You'll know if the form is hot enough when you dip it into the batter and the batter sticks.

Dip hot rosette form into the batter no more than 3/4 it's depth. Immediately plunge into hot oil and cook until the bubbling ceases. Usually the rosettes will fall from the form after cooking a few minutes. If not remove with a fork.

Using a large slotted spatula, remove rosettes from oil as soon as light brown or they begin floating. Place them on paper towels to drain. You'll probably want to practice with a few first, to get the feel of it. While still warm, sift powdered sugar onto the rosette, covering completely.

HOMEMADE SALSA

1 small onion or half medium, diced. Dry out on a paper towel
1 28 oz can whole tomatoes
1 small can diced green chilies
2 green onions, chopped
1 small clove garlic, minced
1/4 teaspoon cumin
1/4 teaspoon coriander
Dash of tobasco
Salt and Pepper to taste

In a blender, add all ingredients and blend quickly just once.
Chill for several hours.

To make a quick guacamole, mash an avocado and add several
tablespoons salsa.

SAUSAGE ROLLS

These little treats were mom's traditional Christmas Eve snack. They work for any occasion, but we usually had them during the holidays. Back when the boys were young like 4 and 6, we established a tradition that we would have Christmas Eve at our house, inviting all the family, hoping everyone would drop by.

During the day, mom and I would cook and bake, planning to be ready by 6:30. Candles always burning, music in the background and the smell of fresh garland set the scene. Tons of decorations and lights were put up along with a giant tree.

Mom would show up dressed in her St. John knit and suede coat, carrying trays of food. Vernon would be right behind her in western boots, belt, and his huge black cowboy hat. Vern had been appointed to bringing in the presents. So sweet just watching the two of them. Mom always smelling of Shalimar, her favorite perfume.

One year Joe (Uncle Sonny) showed up at the door with a huge "HO HO HO" and bells clanging. We all looked out the window and saw this amazing Santa, all in red with a big bag hung over his shoulder. Santa was full of so much cheer, he was a bit tipsy. We barely got the door open before Justin and Matt each had a hand and were dragging him to the chair. Each rattling off their Christmas wish list.

Then, Santa pulled mom to his lap and "HO HO HO" with a drink in hand. Mom got the giggles and brought laughter to us all. There's a picture somewhere of the two of them. Such a beautiful memory for us all.

Just after Santa left for more visits and a little more cheer, Justin mentioned that Santa smelled just like Uncle Sonny. Hmmm...., we left it at that. No one ever said a word.

I wonder what ever happened to that Santa suit.

RECIPE

Preheat oven to 425F

1 beaten egg
1/3 cup fine bread crumbs
1/4 cup finely chopped onion
1 pound bulk pork sausage
1 17 1/2oz pkg frozen puff pastry (thawed)

In a large mixing bowl, combine egg, breadcrumbs onion and sausage. Shape into 8 (5") rolls. Place sausages on a shallow, baking pan and bake for 20 minutes. Remove from oven, drain and cool.

Cut each pastry sheet into 4 quarters. Place each sausage roll on long side of pastry quarter and roll. Seal edges and place on a 15x10x1 baking sheet. Bake for about 20 minutes or until rolls are nicely browned. When cool, cut each roll into 1" slices. Recipe makes 40 pieces.

SCALLOPED POTATOES

Easter or New Year's Day dinners showcased a full baked ham, skin and all. And, there was absolutely never a New Year's dinner without black eyed peas. Mom was raised believing black eyed peas were critical to starting the new year off in prosperity. And a little scalloped potatoes never hurts.

RECIPE

Preheat oven t0 350F. Grease a 2 quart casserole dish.
Line the bottom of the oven with foil, as sauce will spill over.

6 to 8 Yukon gold potatoes, sliced thin. Depending on size you need 4 cups

3 tablespoons butter
3 tablespoons flour
1 1/2 teaspoon salt
1/4 teaspoon pepper
1 1/2 cups milk
1 1/2 cup sharp shredded cheese
1/4 cup finely chopped onion

In a large saucepan over low heat, melt butter and stir in flour, salt and pepper. Add milk a little at a time, stirring continuously with a whisk until all the milk incorporated and smooth and thick. About 5 minutes. Do not boil. Add 1 cup cheese, stir until melted.

Place 1/2 potatoes in a prepared casserole dish. Cover with 1/2 sauce and sprinkle half the onions. Repeat layer. Top with the remaining 1/2 cup cheese. Cover and bake for 1 hour. Uncover and continue baking for another 30 minutes

SOUR DILL HALIBUT

Preheat oven to 375F

1 1/2 pounds halibut filets
8 oz mayonaise
8 oz sour cream
1/2 red onion, chopped
1/2 teaspoon fresh or dried dill weed
1 tablespoon fresh squeezed lemon juice
1 teaspoon Worcestershire sauce
1/8 teaspoon cayenne pepper
1/4 teaspoon salt
1/4 teaspoon minced garlic
1 teaspoon fresh parsley, chopped

1 cup fresh grated, or finely crumbled. sour dough bread crumbs
1/2 cup dry white wine.

Combine all ingredients except the bread crumbs, wine and parsley Whisk together and set aside.

Rinse fish and pat dry with a paper towel. Place filets in a glass baking dish. Pat breadcrumbs on top of fish and sprinkle wine over the breadcrumbs. Pour mayo mixture over each filet, generously.

Bake in preheated oven for about 15-20 minutes, depending on thickness of the filets. Sauce will be golden brown. Sprinkle parsley on top prior to serving.

SOUTHERN PECAN PIE

RECIPE

PREHEAT OVEN TO 350F.
Unbaked pie shell.

1 cup white corn syrup (Karo)
1 cup dark brown sugar
1/3 cup melted butter
1 1/2 cup shelled pecans, while and pieces
3 eggs
1/2 teaspoon vanilla
Dash of salt

Mix all ingredients well and pour into an unbaked pie shell. Bake for 45-50 minutes. Remove from oven and cool.

MOM'S SOUTHERN POTATO SALAD

When we were growing up, I thought all potato salad was like mom's. Wasn't until years later that I learned that wasn't true. Mom was taught to make this salad by her mother. Nothing ever varied in the process. Including, her using an old, completely worn down pairing knife to peel the potatoes. She didn't own a potato peeler. So, I never used one either. Well, until I was married with children and a job. A peeler is so much more efficient and quicker. Plus, I didn't need as many potatoes, as I never really perfected the knife peeling. Even though mom spent a lot of time showing me.

I suppose the potato peeling experience with Mom is what sparked the idea for this little cookbook. I have been so very thankful for the years I shared with mom in the kitchen and the relationship we built around cooking, I have never peeled a potato that I haven't seen moms long fingers and beautiful nails, carefully holding that old knife. Bittersweet memories. I didn't have a daughter to pass down the recipes, stories and traditions that had been handed down from my grandmother. Who would benefit from all those shared experiences, other than myself?

It wasn't so important that the actual recipes be passed on, but the precious moments shared in the kitchen with mom, where I learned all about my grandmother. All the fun, the laughter and those silly mistakes. Truth be told, I believe I hugged and kissed mom more in the kitchen than any other place.

Those experiences just couldn't end with me. There was no daughter to share with, as I completely turned Chelsea off from cooking. But, I did have two sons. Justin and Matt grew up with their grandmother cooking and baking for them, as she did for me. Little pleased mom more than frying up a steak for those boys. Frying anything at my house was out of the question, so most everything at grandma's got fried. I thought maybe they would like to have the opportunity to pass on some of grandma's traditions and make memories of their

own. Or at the very least, they might like being able to read a recipe or two and remember her spirit in the kitchen.

RECIPE

Again, there was no written recipe. So, I made this salad and wrote down the measurements I used. Truthfully, just add more or less of anything according to taste.

I do know that mom believed that Yukon gold were the best potatoes to use. So place 8 whole medium potatoes (similar in size) in a large pot and bring to a boil. Cook for about 20 minutes and check for doneness using a sharp knife. The knife should easily slide into the center. Try not to overcook.

While potatoes are cooking, hard boil 3 eggs. Set aside in cold water.

When potatoes are done, carefully remove from hot water, run under cold water and put in large bowl. Set aside potatoes until they are cool enough to touch. Remove peels while potatoes are still whole. Peels will usually slide off without tearing the potato. Cut each potato into quarters. Then cut each quarter into 4 somewhat equal pieces. Place cut potatoes into a very large mixing bowl. Chop cooked eggs and add to potatoes without mixing yet.

Add the following ingredients

1 medium onion, chopped
3 large celery stalks, chopped
8 sweet pickles, chopped, along with 2 teaspoons of pickle juice
(Or 2 -3 tablespoons sweet relish)
2 tablespoons, or more, yellow mustard
4 tablespoons, or more, Miracle Whip, not real mayo
Salt and Pepper to taste

Mix carefully with a large wooden spoon. Careful not to mash the potatoes. Just add more of anything according to your taste.

GLAZED SALMON
WITH SWEET CHILI SAUCE

I found this recipe while visiting Uncle Sonny in Seattle, October 2020. Joe's friend gifted us with just caught Pacific Northwest salmon. I was excited to make it for dinner, but, Joe isn't really a fan of fish, so he wanted it somewhat disguised. As he loves hot and spicy sauces, I thought this recipe sounded perfect. It was beyond amazing, even for Joe.

RECIPE

1 1/2 pounds of Salmon or four 6 oz pieces
4-6 tablespoons Thai /sweet Chili Sauce. (Best quality is Thai Kitchen or Mae Ploy)
3 Tablespoons soy sauce
3 tablespoons honey (more or less depending on sweetness of chili sauce)
1 tablespoon ginger, freshly grated
1/2 teaspoon ground ginger
Juice of 1/2 lime
2 scallions, sliced

In a shallow backing pan mix all ingredients. Save 1/4 cup marinade for later. Place salmon skin side up into marinade and let marinate for an hour in refrigerator.

Set oven rack 5-6 inches from broiler and preheat.

Line baking sheet with foil, Spray with non stick cooking spray. Transfer salmon to prepared pan, skin side down. Drizzle a little marinade on top. Easy on the marinade so as not to let it pool on baking sheet, or it will burn. Broil salmon for 7-10 minutes, or until fish is just done in center.and is flakey. Try not to overcook, or the fish will be dry Glaze should be carmalized.

Transfer salmon to serving platter and pour reserved sauce on top. Garnish with scallions.

STRAWBERRY RHUBARB PIE
BY GRANDMA ROSE

Well, there's one thing the entire Walsh family could agree on, Grandma Rose made THE BEST strawberry rhubarb pie, hands down. And, she couldn't make them fast enough. Without a doubt, as soon as the pie cooled enough to cut, we fought over getting a slice.

I asked for her recipe and she just smiled and told me she didn't have one. She had no idea of how much of anything she used. Rose could make them in her sleep. We decided to make one together and I guessed at most of the amounts. She believed you could add more or less of anything, depending on taste. Lots of butter is the final ingredient, I know that.

RECIPE

Preheat oven to 400F
Prepare pastry for bottom and top of a 9" pie plate. She never bought a pie crust in her life. There's a scratch one provided in this cookbook. Or, if you're short of time and or energy, I found the Marie Calendar frozen pie crusts are surprisingly good.

1 1/2 cups sugar
3 tablespoons "quick cooking tapioca"
1/2 teaspoon salt
1/4 teaspoon nutmeg
1 pound fresh rhubarb, cut into 1 inch pieces, enough to make 3 cups
1 1/2 cups sliced fresh strawberries
1/2 cup butter

Combine sugar, tapioca, salt and nutmeg together. Mix together to coat fruit. Let stand 20 minutes.

Pour filling into pie crust and dot with butter. Grandma Rose told me that butter was very important for flavor. And, she said just use a whole stick.

Cover with remaining pie crust, or lattice top if preferred. Seal edges and cut small slices in top crust allowing for air to escape as the pie cooks. Bake for about 40 minutes. Let cool and serve warm.

STUFFED PEPPERS

Preheat oven to 400F

1 cup white rice, cooked
6 large peppers (any color) medium to large
1 tablespoon oil
1 small onion, chopped fine
1 small clove garlic, minced
1 pound lean ground beef
2 teaspoons Italian seasoning. (I like to use fresh thyme, rosemary and oregano if i have it on hand)
1 teaspoon salt
1/4 teaspoon pepper
1 15oz can tomato sauce

Make rice ahead of time as per instructions. (1 cup is approximate 1/2 cup uncooked rice and 11/4 cup water.)

Carefully cut stems from peppers and clean out the seeds. Mom always used a spoon to clean out the membranes, careful not to go too deep.

In a square pan place about 1/2 inch of water. Turn peppers upside down in the water, stacking them close. Bake for 20 minutes. Remove from pan, turn right side up. Let cool and set aside for stuffing.

In a large sauce pan heat oil over medium heat. Brown onions and garlic. Push vegetables to side of pan and add ground beef, stirring to break it up in small pieces, searing until brown. Add seasonings and mix well.

Toss cooked rice with meat and half of the tomato sauce. Carefully fill each pepper to the top. Pour remaining sauce over the peppers.

Lower oven to 350. Bake for 40 minutes. If you want to add mozzarella or parmigiana cheese on top, remove the peppers after 20 minutes top with cheese and continue baking for the remaining 20 minutes. Let stand 10 min before serving.

GRANDMA ROSE'S
SWEET POTATO & APPLE CASSEROLE

The is another one of Grandma Rose's infamous dishes. We all enjoyed it every Thanksgiving at her house for as long as I can remember. After we moved to Seattle, I called Rose and asked for the recipe. Way back, when mail was delivered by the mailman, I received it. Like mom, she never measured anything. I'm thinking it was a generation thing. Anyway, I guessed as to the correct amounts. About a week after the recipe arrived, Rose called to say that she woke up remembering she forgot to add the butter to the list of ingredients. As mom believed in adding a lot of love and care to the recipe, Rose believed extra butter made everything better.

RECIPE

Preheat oven to 350F
Butter a large casserole dish

About 8 big sweet potatoes. Try to get those that are dark orange inside.
10-12 Macintosh apples. Try not to use any other apple. Trust me, it won't taste the same.
Sugar
Cinnamon
1 stick butter

Boil the potatoes until not quite done. Drain and cool enough to slice roughly 1/2 inch thick.

While the potatoes are cooking, peel and slice the apples maybe 1/4 inch thick.

Line the bottom of the buttered casserole dish with a layer of potatoes. Sprinkle with sugar and cinnamon. (Grandma said not to use too much cinnamon and about 1 1/2 cup sugar in all.) Next, put a layer

of sliced apples. Again, sprinkle with cinnamon and sugar. Continue layering potatoes and apples, using more apples than potatoes. Cut butter into chucks and place evenly on top of casserole.

Bake for about an hour.

MARMALADE GLAZED SPICY
TEQUILA CHICKEN WINGS

3 pounds uncooked chicken wings or legs and wings

1/2 cup tequila
1/2 cup chopped fresh cilantro
3 tablespoons lime or lemon marmalade
1/4 cup olive oil
2 tablespoons fresh lime juice
1/2 tablespoon coarsely ground pepper
3 medium garlic cloves, minced
1 teaspoon hot pepper sauce
1 teaspoon salt
1/2 teaspoon grated lime peel

Marinate chicken in:
tequila, cilantro, 3 tablespoons marmalade, oil, 2 tablespoons lime juice, pepper, garlic, hot pepper sauce, salt and 1/2 teaspoon lime peel.

Precook chicken meat by frying to baking until just about done. Roughly 15 minutes, depending on thickness.

Pour remaining marinade into a heavy saucepan. Boil until reduced about half. Add remaining 4 tablespoon marmalade, 2 tablespoons lime juice and 1/2 teaspoon lime peel.

Strain marinade into a heavy sauce pan and bring to a boil. Continue boiling until the marinade has been reduced to about half. Remove from heat and add 4 more tablespoons marmalade, an additional 2 tablespoons lime juice and 1/2 teaspoon lime peel.

Brush chicken with more marinade. Grill or broil for about 10 minutes until done.

TRI TIP ROAST

This is one of those recipes Kirkland Costco used to hand out when a specific cut of meat was on sale. (Those days are gone.) And, of course, never wanting to pass up a sale, I just took a chance. It was so delicious! Justin and Matt were crazy over it. So, I made it often when they were in their teens. At some point, I knew the recipe so well, I just started winging it. Eventually making the marinade to my own taste.

The meat was thick and cut into 2 large triangle pieces, like roasts. Unfortunately, when I moved to the East coast, I couldn't find this cut anywhere. I later learned that instead of coming in roast sizes, I found it cut in strips. They tasted the same, just cooked a little quicker. Seattle weather wasn't conducive to a lot of grilling, so I baked it. But, it's wonderful when grilled.

Much like mom, I eventually just started combining whatever ingredients I thought I needed and would give the marinade a taste test. Then, if necessary, I'd just add a bit more of something. But, for the purpose of an actual recipe, t think these measurements are close. Taste test and make it your own.

2 1 1/2 roasts or 4 longer strips of Tri tip

In a roasting pan, whisk together the following ingredients.
1/4 cup oil
3 tablespoons cider vinegar
3 tablespoons low sodium soy sauce
2-3 tablespoons Worcester sauce
1/4 teaspoon kosher salt
1/2 teaspoon pepper.
1/3 cup Kraft Parmesan cheese. Not fresh

At this point you're on your own. Taste a small amount. No one ingredient should stand out more than the other. Just be sure there is a

flavor of the vinegar. Place meat in marinade and pierce with a large fork. Turn the meat over and do the same. Cover the meat with foil and continue to marinate, for at least 30 minutes. I would marinate it for a few hours, turning and piercing the meat often.

Preheat oven to 375F

Using the same pan, bake for approximately 45 minutes, for roasts or 30 minutes for strips. Time varies on how thick the meat is and doneness preferred. I just use a fork and feel for doneness. It's best to undercook, as the meat continues to cook during the 10 minute resting time. We loved the marinade poured over the meat before serving.

I never made this without seasoned roasted potatoes, as the boys loved those too. See recipe included in the cookbook for roasted potatoes.

It's apparent, that over the years in my own kitchen, I was cooking with love for my own family.

TUNA A LA KING

Another very inexpensive and quick dish for dinner I liked to make on a cold, rainy Seattle night.

RECIPE

2 Tablespoons butter
4 tablespoons flour
1 2/3 cups milk, room temperature if possible
1/3 cup half and half or heavy cream
1/4 teaspoon paprika
1/4 teaspoon salt
1/4 teaspoon white pepper

2 eggs, beaten
1 cup frozen peas
1/4 teaspoon celery salt
2 8 oz cans of white tuna in water

*Here is where I mention that mom never bought white tuna in water. She only bought light tuna in oil. So, if you want, you can experiment a little.

First, you need to make the following white sauce.

In a larger heavy pot, melt the butter over low heat. Slowly add the flour and stir to make a thick paste. Very slowly add the milk and cream a little at a time. Cook over medium to low heat, stirring constantly until the sauce thickens. Be careful not to allow the sauce of scorch on the bottom. Add the beaten eggs and continue to cook for about 2 minutes. Last, add the peas, tuna and seasonings. Cook for another 3 minutes to allow peas to thaw and heat up.

Serve over toasted bread or English muffins.

TUNA CASSEROLE

When times were rough, mom would make this inexpensive and quick dinner. Plus we'd have left overs for the next day. Actually, I always thought it tasted better the second day.

Boys, don't be fooled into thinking this recipe is brainless, though it should be. There have been a few boo boos over the years. Remember when we were living in the Kirkland house and I made this for dinner and forgot to put the TUNA in? That created some laughter.

And then there was the time in Kirkland when I went on strike and you kids took turns making dinner. Chelsea was about 13 and she chose this recipe. She made the casserole and we all sat down at the table. When we started eating, we realized that she hadn't precooked the macaroni! We tried not to laugh, but couldn't help it. Chelsea was so hurt. We all felt so sorry. I'm not sure she ever forgave us. I take full responsibility for her deciding never to cook when she got married.

RECIPE

Preheat oven to 350F. Grease a large casserole dish.

1 pound box of elbow macaroni, cooked
2 8oz cans of white tuna in water
1 16oz package frozen mixed vegetables
1/2 cup chopped onion
2 8z cans of mushroom soup
1 cup bread crumbs
2 tablespoons butter, melted

First, cook the elbows as instructed until well done.

Mix all other ingredients together and pour into prepared dish. Top with bread crumbs and melted butter.
Bake 45 minutes, uncovered.

WALNUT DAINTIES

I believe mom used to make these cookies with her mother during the holidays on the farm.

They are so light and airy. They just crumble in your mouth, which is probably why mom loved them so much with black coffee.

RECIPE

Preheat oven to 300

In a large bowl, cream together
1/2 cup butter
2 tablespoons sugar
1 teaspoon vanilla
1/4 teaspoon salt

Add 1 cup all purpose flour, sifted
1/2 cup chopped walnuts

Mix well by hand. Measuring with a full teaspoon, roll mixture into a small ball and then roll into powdered sugar. Place them onto a non greased cookie sheet.

Bake about 40 minutes, or until they are just slightly brown. When cool, roll cookies in powdered sugar again.

YORKSHIRE PUDDING

This is definitely a Brealey tradition. Very British. No holiday was ever celebrated without either Yorkshire puddings or Popovers.

RECIPE for Yorkshire puddings….

The first edition of this cookbook had Nanny's version of these delicate puddings. However, after many years of trying to perfect them, mine always came out FLAT. Many a Thanksgiving, Justin would laugh at how mine didn't look like Nanny's. So, in this version of the cookbook, I'm going to hook you all up!

"HOW TO MAKE YORKSHIRE PUDDINGS, BY JAMIE OLIVER" - YOUTUBE IN 4 MINUTES, YOU'LL HAVE THEM IN THE OVEN AND, BOYS…THEY'RE PERFECT EVERY TIME!!

Just in case you're wanting to try NANNY'S recipe, here it is.

2 cups milk
2 cups flour
4 eggs
1/2 teaspoon salt
Pinch of white pepper
3 tablespoons roast drippings.

Blend all ingredients, other than the drippings, in a 5 cup blender. Blend 5 seconds. Scrape down sides of container and blend again until smooth, 35 to 40 seconds. Cover and refrigerate for an hour.

Preheat oven to 450F

Pour meat drippings in each of the muffin cups in a heavy muffin tin, about 2 tablespoons each. Heat the muffin tin in the oven until dripping are very hot and sizzle. It's critical that the oil is hot enough, or the puddings won't rise. While pan is heating, blend the chilled

batter again for about 5 seconds. Remove hot pan and fill each muffin about 1/2 full of batter. Put back in the oven and reduce heat to 375F. Bake until puddings are double in size and golden brown. Roughly 15 to 20 minutes.

RECIPE for Popovers....

These are much lighter and are basically hollow inside. The only difference is in the ingredients. Baking process is exactly the same.

2 beaten eggs
1 cup milk
1 tablespoon cooking oil
1 cup flour
1/2 teaspoon salt.

Both puddings and popovers are served hot, traditionally served with gravy.

THE DANCE

December 2000

Outside of basketball (even though she was only 5'2") I think mom loved dancing more than anything. She really was a great dancer. She could find the beat in the music and dance to anything. Joe and I would joke that she had more rhythm than the average white woman. Silliness, we knew, but she never got tired of it. Before we were able to dance on our own, mom would swoop us up and swing us around the house, dancing to her favorite tunes. Later, when she felt that we were old enough to hold our own, she taught us how to do the "Twist" and to "Cha Cha". We could feel the music just watching her. There were many times when she and I would be in the kitchen and mom would turn on the radio. We would sing along and dance while waiting for "whatever" to cook.

During our last weekend, mom was losing willpower to converse on any level. Music. I knew she would feel the music. I opened my computer and found an old favorite of hers, "Your Precious Love", by Jerry Butler. As the music began, Joe walked across the room to where mom was seated on the sofa. He bent forward, reached for her hand and asked her to dance. She managed that sweet smile as he helped her up. She carefully placed her tiny bare feet on top of Joe's white socks. There it was, that bond that mothers have with their sons. I could feel it as she looked up into his eyes. In her old, tattered' blue peignoir, mom laid her head on Joe's chest. The dance began. For those few tender moments, there was no cancer, no pain, no heartache. Only the beautiful memories, pushing the fear away, for a snap shot in time. Only her youth and beauty were real.

Floating on the dance floor with her son. A gift for the both of them. On the edge of life, she just let go and one more time, she was lost in the music. Mom was truly a beautiful woman, wife, mother and

grandmother. Rita was an inspiration not only to her family, but to everyone she met. We were blessed.
Let the memories start now.

In her own words…

"Enjoy every moment", "There's happiness to be found, if you look for it.", "God has a plan for us", "You never know what's around the corner". "Just wait and see", and my favorite, "Where is your faith, be patient. God knows what he's doing".